Study Guide

Inside the SAT

Getting Ready for the PSAT | SAT

Doorway to College™ Foundation

Supporting the transition to higher education

ACKNOWLEDGMENTS

Author: Douglas J. Paul, Ph.D.

Editorial Team: James A. Bartlett, Karen Nichols, Julia Wasson, Todd Hamer, Terry Meier, Gary Hirsch, Charles Collins, Renee Zukin

Graphic Design: Kelli Cerruto

Cover Design: Christopher Reese

CONTRIBUTORS

Acknowledgment of Contributions: The presenters of several thousand seminars have contributed their time and energy to the continuing evolution and improvement of this program since its origin in 1985. Special recognition goes to Rick Adler, Diana Anderson, Marty Barrett, Jim Bartlett, Lyn Benedict, Dennis Benson, Carol Braker, Debara Burke, Kaye Byrnes, Joe Carney, Esther Caudle, Henry Caudle, Coral Chilcote, Sheila Cocke, Shari Cornelison, Josh Crittenden, Brian Crouch, Kyra Curtis, Matthew Dahmen, Howard DeWild, Christine Edmunds, Patricia Fremarek, Bob Gould, Sue Grohn, Susan Hamel, Zack Hamingson, Steve Hausauer, Liz Higgins, Gary Hirsch, Pamela Hughes, Clint Huntrods, Marilyn Jackson, Rick Kemmer, Hildred Lewis, Kerri Mabee, Wanda Martinez, Wendy Mattingly, Esther McGuire, Jay Meier, Terry Meier, Dan Mohwinkel, Pat Mooney, Michael Morgan, Deb Oronzio, Jane Petersen, Jim Petersen, Gareth Reagan, Dan Ryan, Kim Stanley, Tom Stirling, Laura Stolpe, Milton Strange, Dan Thorstenson, Linda Usrey, Linda Welp, Audra Yokley.

In addition, guidance officers and administrators in hundreds of school districts have provided data for the research basis of the program strategies and focus. We also thank the more than 500,000 students who have offered their personal evaluation of the seminar and given their comments for areas of weakness and strength.

ABOUT DOORWAY TO COLLEGE FOUNDATION

Doorway to College Foundation strives to demystify the college application process in its many forms. We give parents and students the information needed to be fully informed and prepared for the challenges and changes that lie on the horizon. For more information about Doorway to College Foundation's products and services, visit **www.doorwaytocollege.com**.

3106 Rochester Avenue
Iowa City, Iowa 52245
P: 877.928.8378
F: 319.499.5289

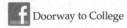 Doorway to College   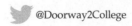 @Doorway2College   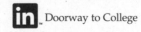 Doorway to College   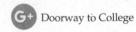 Doorway to College

10 9 8 7 6

ISBN: 978-1-941219-08-9

Contents

Introduction

You can't do better than to reach your highest potential. If you get the best possible score you can achieve on the PSAT or the SAT, you deserve it, and you should be proud of it.

Unfortunately, not everybody reaches their highest potential. There are many reasons why this happens. Sometimes people don't know what to expect on the test. They don't know the best way to attack the test. Anxiety makes them freeze up. They just don't prepare well. Or they set their expectations too low.

The goal of this book is to help you reach your highest potential score on the PSAT and/or SAT. It was developed to help you get over the obstacles that can keep you from getting there. No matter how high you climb on the score scale, if it's the very best you're capable of, you shouldn't be disappointed with it.

Please note: The PSAT and SAT are essentially the same test, with very few differences. Unless otherwise stated, when we refer to the SAT, we are referring to both tests. The College Board is the publisher of the PSAT and SAT.

Objectives of *Inside the SAT*

1. To demystify the PSAT and SAT

In order to attain your personal best, you need to know as much as possible about the PSAT and SAT. This program will give you insights into how the tests are constructed. It will expose you to the types of questions you can expect to see on the test, the difficulty levels you should expect, and the content you need to master.

2. To reduce test anxiety and its negative effects on your scores

A standardized testing situation tends to create a high level of anxiety. Test anxiety can be a major negative factor when it comes to maintaining your concentration. One objective of *Inside the SAT* is to help you know what to expect from each part of the test. This familiarity breeds a confidence that helps reduce test anxiety. A calm but focused mind will allow you to concentrate on finding the correct answers, rather than fighting off a serious case of anxiety.

3. To teach both general and specific strategies for taking multiple-choice tests

Inside the SAT covers numerous strategies for taking multiple-choice tests. Some of these methods will become tools that you will apply to other multiple-choice tests you encounter in high school and college. Other strategies are specific to the types of questions that appear only on the PSAT and SAT. Other than the essay, which is only given on the SAT, all strategies and tips in this book apply to both the PSAT and SAT, even where "SAT" is the only test mentioned.

Nobody needs help on a test when the answers are obvious. The emphasis of *Inside the SAT* is on what to do when the correct answer is not immediately apparent. The strategies for attacking difficult questions will transfer to other testing situations throughout your career as a student.

Chapter 1

The PSAT and SAT

Here are a few things to know about the PSAT.

The PSAT is the qualifying exam for the National Merit Scholarship Program, which is why it's also known as the NMSQT (National Merit Scholarship Qualifying Test). It's hard to qualify for a National Merit Scholarship, and only a small percentage of students who take the test do so—but if you have the academic skills to do it, you should definitely take the PSAT.

Even if you don't think you'll become a National Merit Scholar, taking the PSAT is still a good idea. It's great practice for the SAT. If you know you're going to take the SAT at some point in the future, take the PSAT first. It's a way of practicing for the SAT under real test conditions, without the pressure some students feel when taking the SAT itself.

The PSAT is only offered in the month of October and there is no make-up date if you miss the test date. Check with your school counselor to see when the test is offered so you can plan ahead. If you have a 504 Plan or an Individualized Education Plan (IEP), you may be eligible to take the test under special conditions but you must apply to College Board early.

Now, what about the SAT?

The SAT is one of the two major college entrance exams; the ACT is the other. Most students enrolling in college each year take one test; some students take both. The SAT is very much like the PSAT, but longer.

In 2014, the College Board, the organization that publishes the SAT and PSAT, announced a major revision of the tests for the 2015–2016 school year and beyond. This Study Guide is appropriate for these new tests.

What's on the Test?

The PSAT and SAT say they have two sections, but as far as you're concerned, the PSAT has three, and the SAT has four:

- Evidence-Based Reading and Writing (in two parts, **Reading** and **Writing**, which you will take separately)
- **Math**
- **Essay** (only on the the SAT, and optional)

The reading section contains a series of passages followed by questions. The writing section gives you a series of passages with bits that are underlined. Your job is to examine the underlined bit, determine if it's right, and choose the correct fix if it isn't.

The math section contains a mix of multiple-choice and open-ended problems. The SAT math test is supposed to reflect what students do in high school math classes—and what you will be expected to do in first-year college math classes.

The PSAT doesn't have an essay. The SAT essay is optional, but the option to use it lies with colleges. They may require the essay for incoming students or they may not. The essay requires students to read a passage by another writer and then evaluate the quality of the writer's argument. If you are only concerned with the PSAT right now, you don't have to worry about writing the essay. Yet, the instruction in this book still has value for you, as it will help you understand complex essay assignments like those you'll be required to do in the next few years of school.

The PSAT runs two hours and 45 minutes, compared to three hours for the SAT. Students writing the SAT essay will spend an extra 50 minutes doing that.

Scoring the Test

On the SAT and PSAT, two section scores are reported: one for Evidence-Based Reading and Writing together and one for Math. Here's how the scoring looks for the two tests.

Test	Reading/Writing Perfect Score	Math Perfect Score	Total Perfect Score	Essay
PSAT	760	760	1520	None
SAT	800	800	1600	Reported separately

If you take the PSAT, you won't get an essay score. If you choose to write the SAT essay, that score will be reported separately from your other scores. We'll talk more about the essay in Chapter 4.

A Note about Timed Tests

Like many competitive events, all of the PSAT and SAT subtests are timed. Many students who have the skills necessary to eventually find all of the right answers do poorly only because of a timing problem.

Wear a Watch to the Test!

The first thing to do at the start of each test section is to write down the time that it will end. The people who administer the test (the proctors) are instructed to announce when you have five minutes left. They are also free to write the start and stop time on the board. Don't count on them—they may fail to give you this courtesy.

Many of the test-taking strategies in this book will require you to be aware of the time all the way through the test, not just at the end. So when the proctor tells you what time the test will end, *write it down*.

Write the stop time on the front cover of your test booklet. If you write it somewhere in the middle of the booklet, you will have to flip to find it. Although you'll need to turn to the cover to see the time, at least you'll be able to do this quickly.

> At the start of EVERY test, write down the time for completion. This is an easy place to establish control.

Many students think they will simply remember the stop time. Don't try it. When you are concentrating on the test, it's very difficult to keep timing in mind and still do your best work. Write it down.

Guessing

Never, ever, for any reason, leave any blanks on the PSAT and SAT. Blind guessing cannot hurt you—it can only help you.

> If you leave blanks on this test, you are throwing away points.

Whenever possible, eliminate choices *before* you guess. By learning ways to eliminate wrong choices, you can significantly increase your score.

ZAPPING

Doorway to College Foundation has developed a strategy for "zeroing-in" on the right answer before picking. It's called *ZAPPING*. The exact method of *ZAPPING* is different for each type of question on the PSAT and SAT.

Zero-in And Pick

For all of the subtests on the PSAT and SAT:

1) If you know the answer, answer the question.

2) If you don't know the answer, *ZAP* before you guess.

3) If you can't *ZAP*, then make a blind guess.

How Does *ZAPPING* Work?

The difficulty of a multiple-choice question isn't really in the question. It's in the wrong answer choices you're given. The point of the wrong choices is to hide the right answer.

Here's a sample test question.

> Which scientist won a Nobel Prize in 1903 for the discovery of radium?
> A) Albert Einstein
> B) Marie Curie
> C) Gregor Mendel
> D) Michael Faraday

Which of these four famous scientists is known for discovering radium? If you know, that's great, but if you don't, this question is pretty hard. If you guess at it, you have a 75 percent chance of being wrong.

But what if we changed the question to make it a little easier?

> Which scientist won a Nobel Prize in 1903 for the discovery of radium?
> A) Albert Einstein
> B) Marie Curie
> C) Theodore Roosevelt
> D) Bill Gates

The question is the same, but a couple of the choices are different. You can *ZAP* Theodore Roosevelt because he's not a scientist, and you can *ZAP* Bill Gates because he's alive at the time this book was written—which someone who won a Nobel Prize in 1903 would not be. Now you only need to consider two choices. If you have to guess, you have a 50-50 chance of being right.

We'll say it again: The difficulty of a multiple-choice question is in the *wrong choices*. When the choices are all similar, like the pioneers of science in the first example, the question can be hard to get right. When there's more differentiation in your mind between the choices, the question becomes easier to get right. The greater the differences between the choices, the easier the question becomes.

Here's an example of what we mean:

Which scientist won a Nobel Prize in 1903 for the discovery of radium?
A) LeBron James
B) Marie Curie
C) Homer Simpson
D) Beyoncé

Now the right answer to the question should be obvious to everyone.

Some of the questions on the PSAT and SAT will contain at least one answer choice that's every bit as far-fetched as Bill Gates or Beyoncé. If you can spot those choices on the questions that are the most difficult for you and eliminate them, your odds of finding the right answer (or correctly guessing it) will go way up.

ZAPPING is a powerful tool that lets you use your partial knowledge to screen out wrong answers and narrow the choices. You might not know who won a Nobel Prize for the discovery of radium, but if you know who *didn't*, you can use that knowledge to get the question right—or at a minimum, to increase the odds of getting it right.

So don't be afraid to use the *ZAPPING* technique—or to take a guess anywhere on the test. Sure, you'll make some wrong guesses, but don't worry about it, because they'll be on questions you have a lesser chance of getting right anyway. You can't hurt your score by *ZAPPING*, because there's no penalty for getting a question wrong. And if you guess right, it counts just like you knew the answer all along.

Incredibly Important, Not-to-Be-Underestimated Tip

You'll learn a lot of strategies and tips in this program. They'll all help you if you apply them. But the most important is one of the simplest: Leave no blanks!

If you leave blanks on the test, you are throwing away points. So, *ZAP* when you can, then guess on what remains. It can only help your score.

General Tips

Based on our work with thousands of students, we want to address some common questions and share a little general information. *Inside the SAT* was developed with insights that our editorial staff had from developing numerous statewide testing programs. We discovered that when we taught students what we taught our new editors, their scores started to increase.

Using that idea, we isolated a few strategies that seemed to have an immediate impact on scores. Over the years, we developed other strategies that have proven to be especially effective with additional practice.

Just so you're straight on this issue, there isn't any strategy or technique that will do the work for you. The score increase that you realize will be a direct result of your personal effort. If you want a higher score, you're going to have to work for it. (Sometimes reality is hard to take.)

The test editors do not intentionally create trick questions.

The PSAT and SAT editors work hard to get rid of trick questions so they never they make it to a final form of the test. Trick questions that get by the editors are nearly always thrown out after a field test. So don't think the test is purposely trying to trick you.

The main point of standardized tests is to separate students with a lot of knowledge from students with less knowledge. Trick questions don't help achieve this goal, so professional test developers do not intentionally include them on their tests.

The test editors really do want to measure your writing, reading, and math abilities. But test writing is as much an art as it is a science, and you might find one or two bad questions.

There is only one right answer to each multiple-choice item.

The test writers go to great lengths to make sure that every multiple-choice item has one—and only one—correct answer. You do not need to worry about having to make extremely fine distinctions between choices. If you feel that two choices for a particular item seem correct, pick the better one. If you can't decide on the better one, pick the one you think the SAT editors would want to see. Don't waste time arguing with yourself.

There is no identifiable pattern of correct answers.

Professional test developers are careful about making sure that the correct answers do not form a predictable pattern on the answer sheet. Many students waste time thinking, *Let's see. I haven't answered D) for about 10 questions, so I'll pick D) for this one.* Even if there were a perfect pattern of answers, the only way to see the pattern would be to answer every item correctly. And, even if you answered as few as one-fourth of the questions incorrectly, a perfect pattern would look totally random.

Some students look for patterns whenever they run into a guessing situation. *Let's see now*, they reason, *I haven't picked D for about eight or nine questions, so I'll guess D on this one.* Sound familiar? Don't waste time trying to track patterns because there simply aren't any. The important aspect of this tip is that you should not waste time looking for a pattern.

All choices are equally likely.

Any particular choice (A, B, C, or D) has an equal chance of being the correct answer. Educational research shows that teacher-made tests often have more Bs and Cs than As and Ds. This is not true of professionally developed standardized tests. The correct answers are distributed relatively equally among the answer choices.

The directions are the same on every form of the test.

Don't spend time reading directions on test day; know them before you go. Use all of the available time to work on the questions.

Write in the test booklet as you take the test.

Many students are hesitant to write in their test booklets because they have been taught not to write in school books. In order to get your best score, you need to write directly in the test booklet. Get into this habit when you take the Workouts.

Write anything that you feel will improve your performance on the test. Here are examples of the kinds of things you should write in your test booklet:

- At the *beginning* of every test, **write down the time** when the test will be over. Then you can pace yourself and control your use of time.
- **Underline keywords** and make other notes that help you understand questions and passages.
- **Mark questions you are skipping** or want to come back to later so you can easily spot them.
- **Cross out the letter** of choices that you *ZAP*.
- Always **circle your answer choice** in the test book, then transfer your answer to the answer sheet. This procedure reduces your chances of mismarking your answer sheet.

In practice, focus on strategy, not score.

Your score will take care of itself. Don't fret about it. Instead, put your attention on strategy. When you practice, don't spend any brain power worrying about whether you're picking up enough skill to raise your score. Just focus on learning and practicing what you learn. Even when you're in the testing center, concentrate on *taking* the test, not on the outcome.

Chapter 2

The Evidence-Based Writing Test

The Writing and Language section of the Evidence-Based Writing Test is really an editing test. (You don't have to actually write anything.) You'll be given four written passages, each of which has several bits underlined. Your job is to pick the correct way to rewrite the underlined bit. Keep in mind that some of the underlines will be correct as they appear, and the correct answer on those will be NO CHANGE.

The Writing and Language section will also include a sprinkling of graphs, charts, and/or tables. You won't be correcting the English used in them, but you will be asked how to incorporate information from the graphic into the text. This is the kind of thing you often do when you're writing a paper—taking quantitative information from a source and deciding how you should write about it—so it shouldn't seem unfamiliar to you.

What to Expect

The Writing and Language Test will cover a wide variety of skills.

Test	Passages	Questions	Minutes
PSAT	4	44	35
SAT	4	44	35

- **Sentence conventions:** fragments, run-ons, subordination and coordination of clauses, parallel structure, placement of modifiers, verb tense, and pronoun shift
- **Usage conventions:** pronouns and possessives, agreement, frequently confused words, comparatives and superlatives, and idiomatic English
- **Punctuation conventions:** end punctuation, punctuation within sentences, possessives, series, nonrestrictive and parenthetical elements, and fixing unnecessary punctuation
- **Expression of ideas:** support, focus, topic sentences
- **Organization:** logical sequence, introductions, conclusions, and transitions
- **Effective language use:** precise language, concise language, style, tone, and syntax

11

Strategy Tips

 tip 1   **Take control of the combined SAT Reading and Writing and Language sections.**

The first step in taking control of the SAT Reading and Writing and Language sections is to shorten both subtests to fit your personal situation. It makes no difference if you score your points on the Reading section or the Writing and Language section. The sections are combined to get your SAT score, and a point on one section counts the same as a point on the other.

If your starting score is around 400, don't fantasize about moving up to a 600. Instead, think in terms of moving up gradually. The number of problems you need to work and double-check depends on your target score. The following table shows what you need to do to hit various target levels.

Reasonable Target SAT Reading & Writing Score	To take control of the Reading & Writing and Language Test, you need to be . . .
790–800	correct on 50 Reading questions and 44 Writing questions. You need to ZAP and then guess on the 2 remaining questions.
710–730	correct on 40 Reading questions and 40 Writing questions. You need to ZAP and then guess on the 16 remaining questions.
610–630	correct on 30 Reading questions and 30 Writing questions. You need to ZAP and then guess on the 36 remaining questions.
510–530	correct on 20 Reading questions and 20 Writing questions. You need to ZAP and then guess on the 56 remaining questions.
430–450	correct on 10 Reading questions and 10 Writing questions. You need to ZAP and then guess on the 76 remaining questions.
380–400	correct on 5 Reading questions and 5 Writing questions. You need to ZAP and then guess on the 86 remaining questions.

For example, if your reasonable target is an SAT Reading & Writing Section score of 520, you need to use as much time as necessary to work and double check 20 of the 52 Reading questions and 20 of the 44 Writing questions—even if it takes nearly all of your test time. In the remaining minutes of each section, ZAP and then guess on the other 56 questions. (32 Reading and 24 Writing). On average, you'll pick the right answer about 14 times out of 56 blind guesses. Using the SAT Conversion Tables, you estimated SAT Score will be about 520.

The key to making this system work is to be perfect on the number of problems that you work and double-check. Careless mistakes can ruin your SAT Score.

Carefully read the entire sentence, not just the underlined part.

You will need to establish a context for the underlined part of the sentence. To do that, be sure to read every word. The questions in this section are asking you to look at the sentences as a whole. Although you may change only the underlined part, be aware that the parts that are *not* underlined will often help you determine the correct answer.

As soon as you realize that a change is needed, immediately *ZAP* NO CHANGE. Then apply your skills to figure out what is wrong and how to fix it.

You can edit only the underlined portion.

Even though you need to read the entire sentence, you can't change anything but the underlined portion. Anything not underlined has to stay as it is. So don't waste time considering how to improve anything that doesn't have a line under it.

That said, be sure to pay attention to how the underlined parts are connected to the parts that aren't underlined. For example, if you see a section that is underlined and it's followed by punctuation that *isn't* underlined, you'd better consider the existing punctuation when you choose the correct fix. Otherwise, you might be fixing one error only to create a new one.

If the sentence sounds correct as is, pick NO CHANGE.

When you see a sentence that contains an underline, read it silently so you can "hear" it in your head. Does it sound awkward? Does it seem too long? Do you feel like it's just not right in some indefinable way? Or does it sound good as it is?

If the underlined part seems okay to you, choose NO CHANGE. It will be the correct answer about one out of four times.

Think how you'd fix the text before you check the choices.

Questions on the Writing and Language section can quickly confuse you if you look at the choices too soon. If it sounds like something is wrong in the sentence, *think about how you could fix it—and whether you should change it at all—before you look at the answer choices.* (Cover them with your hand if that helps you.)

Then look at the choices. There will probably be an answer choice that's close to the fix you thought of.

Read the sentence again. If it seems right, choose that answer and move on. If it doesn't, try one of the others. If none of the choices seems to fit, pick NO CHANGE.

Before you commit to an answer, plug it in and say the sentence in your head.

This strategy is worth the extra time. It's a safety step to avoid making careless mistakes. Before committing to an answer, verbalize the choices in your head. Which one sounds best? Plug it into the sentence in place of the underlined portion. Does it fit when you consider the context of the whole sentence? Then that's most likely your answer.

Time is short; keep moving through the test.

A big part of taking control of the test is to keep your pace in mind. You'll have four passages to do in 35 minutes. That's an average of only 8.75 minutes to read a passage and answer 11 questions about it. Both accuracy and speed will be important in gaining your personal best score.

As you practice, occasionally time yourself on a passage set. Set a timer for 9 minutes and begin reading the selection. Are you finished answering the questions by the time the timer goes off? How fast can you read and still answer the questions correctly?

That theoretical question gets us to the next tip.

Three out of four might be right for you.

If it's difficult for you to read a passage and answer 11 questions in the limited time available to you, you might be wise to quit trying. No, don't give up on the test. What we're talking about is limiting your most serious efforts to three out of the four passages. Focus on doing your very best on those three. Get as many of the answers right as you possibly can.

At that point, go to the fourth passage. *ZAP* any obvious wrong answers as quickly as you can. Guess the rest, filling a bubble for every question. Next, go back and read the fourth passage. Skim it if you have to. Then quickly answer as many of the questions you guessed on as you can; carefully erase the wrong answers and fill in the correct ones as you go.

Working only three passages sounds counterintuitive, doesn't it? You're supposed to read all four passages. Yet, if that doesn't work to your advantage, why would you do it?

But wait! What if you're a gifted reader who can whip through all four passages and get every answer correct with time to spare? By all means, go for it! After all, reading each passage and answering every question is the only way to earn a perfect score.

Grammar and Usage Tips

That/which is not human.

You may be presented with items requiring you to choose among *that*, *which*, *who*, or *whom*. For this tricky usage issue, remember these easy rules:

- Use *that* to introduce clauses with no commas (restrictive clauses) when talking about non-humans.
- Use *which* to introduce clauses with commas (nonrestrictive clauses) when talking about non-humans.
- Use *who* or *whom* when introducing relative clauses referring to humans.

For example:

Political cartoons *that* make fun of lawmakers and politicians can be useful tools in a democratic society.

>   **That** refers to *cartoons*—a non-human.

Political cartoons, *which* make fun of lawmakers and politicians, can be useful tools in a democratic society.

>   **Which** refers to *cartoons*.

Political cartoonists, *who* draw cartoons making fun of lawmakers and politicians, can be useful tools in a democratic society.

>   **Who** refers to *cartoonists*—humans.

Illustrators for whom politics is the focus are generally called political cartoonists.

>   **Whom** refers to *illustrators*—another category of humans.

Is it *better* or *best*?

Some sentences may make you choose between *better* or *best*. Remember this easy guideline:

Between two choices pick the better, among three or more choices pick the best.

To pick the correct choice, simply track the number of things being compared.

For example:

Director Milos Forman received Academy Awards for *One Flew Over the Cuckoo's Nest* and *Amadeus*; it is difficult to say which is the **better** of the two films.

Out of all five of Milos Forman's films, the critics liked *One Flew Over the Cuckoo's Nest* **best**.

Should it be *who* or *whom*?

Chances are, you may be confused about when to use *who* versus *whom*. Think of it this way: *Who* is a pronoun representing a person who is doing an action (the subject). *Whom* is also a pronoun, but *whom* is the object of the action. If you could logically substitute *he* in the sentence, use *who*. If you would logically substitute *him*, use *whom*.

Here's an example:

Whom does my dog like? My dog likes *him*.

Who has a dog? *He* does.

The same rule holds true for *whom* and *her*, but it's easier to remember when both words end in *m*.

Words may sound alike but have very different meanings.

We all misuse even the simplest of words in our day-to-day speech and writing. For example, have you ever replaced *its* for *it's* when writing? Or used *to* when you meant *too*? Sure you have. We all do if we're not paying close attention—and sometimes even when we are. Words that sound alike but are spelled differently are *homophones*. (Don't worry; you don't need to know that bit of information.)

Can you add a few more <u>homophones</u> to the list below?

ascent . . . . . assent	sight . . . . . . site	
cereal. . . . . . serial	stationary . . stationery	
fair. . . . . . . fare	they're. . . . . their . . . . . . there	
it's . . . . its	_____	_____	_____
palate . . . . . palette. . . . . pallet	_____	_____	_____
pore. . . . . . . pour . . . . . . poor	_____	_____	_____
principal. . . principle	_____	_____	_____
sew . . . . so. . . . . sow	_____	_____	_____

Homophones aren't the only words to be concerned about. Watch out for other words that sound very similar to each other but that are quite different indeed.

> Here are some examples of commonly confused words:
>
> access . . . . . excess   form . . . . . . forum
>
> adverse. . . . averse   skeptic . . . . septic
>
> affect . . . . . . effect   than. . . . . . . then
>
> ask. . . . . ax   tortuous . . . torturous
>
> ensure. . . . . insure
>
> Which words do *you* confuse?
>
> _____   _____
>
> _____   _____
>
> _____   _____

If you're not confident that you'll be able to differentiate between these common words when they appear on the test, check out the **ZAPS College Vocabulary Challenge**. The Challenge presents more than 400 college-level words, defines them with synonyms, gives antonyms and roots where appropriate, and tests you in two different ways for each word. You can learn more at **www.doorwaytocollege.com/college-vocabulary-challenge**.

Prepositions are *not* interchangeable.

Be aware of the prepositions that typically accompany certain words. On the SAT, you may see a word that makes perfect sense in an answer choice, but it may be followed by an incorrect preposition. That's a trap. Watch for it.

For example, you might see something like this:

> Billie was <u>averse of</u> turning in his homework earlier than absolutely necessary.
> A) NO CHANGE
> B) adverse at
> C) adverse of
> D) averse to

In this case, the correct answer is D. The word *averse* is always followed by the word *to*.

Were you confused about which word to choose? That's not surprising, because there's a negative tone to each of them. But they're definitely different.

Averse applies to a person and means having a feeling of *distaste, disinclination*, or *resistance*. *Adverse* applies to conditions or circumstances that are *hostile, unfavorable*, or *contrary*. For example, "The launch was delayed due to *adverse* weather conditions." The word *adverse* can't be applied to a human.

tip 6 Avoid redundancy.

One thing the SAT will likely test is whether you can identify redundancies. A redundancy is saying the same thing twice (or more times) in the same sentence. Redundant writing is bad and poor writing. It's also incorrect and wrong writing. (Yes, we, too, can be redundant!) Look in the gray box to see examples of redundancies that you may be using in your own speech and writing. Watch and look out for them!

The SAT editors can be tricky when testing redundancies. They don't necessarily put the redundancies next to each other, but the redundant words will be in the same sentence. For example, you might see an underlined sentence like the following:

The severe weather siren <u>gave a warning to the community in advance</u>.

A) NO CHANGE

B) warned the community in advance.

C) warned the community.

D) gave an advance warning to the community.

What's the best answer? A *warning* is something that you would give *before* something bad happens. So, by definition, a warning occurs in *advance*. The answer is C.

Here are a few common examples of redundancy. Can you figure out what makes each pair redundant? As you hear others or recognize them in your own speech, add them to this list. And watch for them on the test!

absolute necessity	end result	new beginning	sugary sweet
actual fact	extract out	past memories	surrounded on all sides
advance planning	final conclusion	pick and choose	
and also	first introduced	plan in advance	tiny bit
blend together	join together	regular routine	true facts
bow down	kneel down	safe sanctuary	unexpected surprise
circle around	lift up	same exact	unintentional mistake
connect together	local residents	small speck	usual custom
drop down	mental telepathy	sudden impulse	vacillate back and forth

_____ _____ _____ _____

_____ _____ _____ _____

Form possessives with care.

Following are basic rules for forming possessives. You likely learned them in elementary school or middle school, but you may not remember them well enough without a bit of review. Study these examples. Commonplace as they seem, you may well be tested on possessives like these.

Singular Noun	Singular Possessive Example	Plural Noun	Plural Possessive Example
pen	pen's cap	pens	pens' caps
map	map's legend	maps	maps' legends
Ellen Quince	Ellen Quince's house	the Quinces	the Quinces' house
dress	the dress's button	dresses	the dresses' buttons
Ms. James	Ms. James's book	the Jameses	the Jameses' books

Are you tracking *among* choices or *between* choices?

Look for sentences that force you to choose either *among* or *between*. If your 8th-grade English teacher taught you to remember "between two and among three," then you learned a simple rule for a complex grammatical issue. Although many textbooks agree with the simple rule, the most authoritative source for correct English, *The Oxford English Dictionary*, cites the following source:

> In all senses *between* has been, from its earliest appearance, extended to more than two. . . It is still the only word available to express the relation of a thing to many surrounding things severally and individually. —*The Rhinehart Guide to Grammar*, page 380

For example:

Sparta, the fiercest of the ancient Greek city-states, imposed rigorous military training upon every male **between** the ages of seven and sixty.

The treaty **between** France, Italy and Russia was ill fated from its conception due to outside pressures from the Germans.

So when can you use *between*? Pretty much whenever it sounds okay. The people who write the SAT would have a hard time refusing an answer that is supported by *The Oxford English Dictionary*.

But what about *among*? The use of this word is much more restricted. For this reason, therefore, it is more likely to be tested. (Standardized-test writers don't like controversy. No surprise there.) *Among* is best used when it suggests a relationship of someone or something to a surrounding group. It is *not* a good word to use when comparing only two things.

For example:

> In an effort to learn about South American gold-mining practices, the anthropologist lived **among** the miners for five years.

Watch out for sentence fragments.

Incomplete sentences (fragments) are a frequent occurrence in student writing, so the problem is likely to appear on this part of the test. A fragment is a group of words that does not express a complete thought. A complete sentence requires both a subject and a verb. If either part is missing, the sentence is incomplete and must be corrected.

This can happen with a lot of words as easily as with only a few. In other words, you might come across long sentence fragments, not just short ones.

For example:

> Running and jumping in new <u>sneakers and kicking at</u> an anthill to see what we could stir up.
>
> A) NO CHANGE
>
> B) sneakers and kicking at
>
> C) sneakers; and kicking at
>
> D) sneakers, we would kick at

The example is a fragment because it's missing a subject. Choice D fixes the error.

It's true that many writers of fiction and literary nonfiction use fragments. A lot. (We just did.) And that's perfectly okay in the right piece. But it's definitely not okay on the SAT. If you see a fragment in the Writing and Language section, immediately *ZAP* NO CHANGE. It's wrong. And no amount of arguing with those who wrote the test will get them to call it right. Really.

Shorter is (usually) better.

The test is looking for clear, concise language. If a sentence is grammatically correct, then leave it alone. In order to be relevant, additional text must either add new information or clarify existing information. Do not fall into the trap of picking longer, wordier choices just because you think they sound more intelligent. Make sure any additional wording serves a purpose; if it doesn't, don't pick it.

In the following example, choices B, C, and D offer wordier solutions to a sentence that is correct as is.

Cockroaches were the predominant insects 300 million years <u>ago and are likely to survive</u> into the next era of geologic time.

A) NO CHANGE

B) ago; and they are more than likely to survive

C) ago, and it is still likely they could survive

D) ago; still, they would be likely to survive

Shorter isn't always better—sometimes the shortest option leaves out necessary information. But after you have applied all the content knowledge you possess and all the other tips you remember, if you still can't get down to a single answer choice, the odds are in your favor if you pick the shortest choice. But choose that strategy only when you're guessing.

Be sure modifiers are placed correctly.

The test will have questions intended to determine whether you can place modifiers in the right spot, as close as possible to whatever the phrase is intending to modify. Look at this sentence.

Conducting slaves to freedom on the Underground Railroad, <u>danger continually stalked Harriet Tubman</u>.

Take a look at the phrase "conducting slaves to freedom on the Underground Railroad." Based on where it appears in the sentence, it looks like it's describing or modifying *danger*. But does it make sense to say that danger is conducting slaves to freedom? It does not. It's more likely that the phrase is intended to modify *Harriet Tubman*. Let's look at the choices on the next page and see what our options are.

Conducting slaves to freedom on the Underground Railroad, <u>danger continually stalked Harriet Tubman</u>.

A) NO CHANGE

B) stalked Harriet Tubman.

C) Harriet Tubman and danger were continually stalked.

D) Harriet Tubman was continually stalked by danger.

Let's take it choice by choice. We already know we don't like the sentence as it is, so let's *ZAP* choice A. Choice B makes a sentence fragment. Choice C puts *Harriet Tubman* in the right place now, but *danger* is misplaced.

If we've *ZAPPED* all three choices, the one that's left must be correct. But read the answer to yourself to be sure. "Conducting slaves to freedom on the Underground Railroad, Harriet Tubman was continually stalked by danger." Sounds good. Keep it.

By the way, choice B is an example of an answer choice where "Shorter is better" is *not* the correct strategy.

Take note of clause arrangement.

Once again, this test is looking for sentences that are to the point and clear in their meaning. When considering clause arrangement, follow this general rule: Keep the clause as close as possible to what it is modifying. A sentence can use clause structure to strengthen its effectiveness.

For example:

Weaker: Joyce Carol Oates is one of the most prolific writers alive today; she has published more than 100 books of fiction, poetry, and criticism.

Stronger: Having published more than 100 books of fiction, poetry, and criticism, Joyce Carol Oates is one of the most prolific writers alive today.

In the first example, a semicolon separates "one of the most prolific writers" from the number of her publications. In the second example, both the number of publications and the phrase "one of the most prolific writers" are separated only by a comma.

There's nothing inherently wrong with the first sentence, but the second sentence is clearer. The only time you're likely to see a question that pairs two or more correct ways to express a thought is when you're being tested on style and effective language use.

Study proper use of semicolons, commas, and conjunctions.

Each of these elements serves a very different purpose, and they are not interchangeable. The Grammar Review on pages 32–41 of this book will help. If you still aren't 100 percent clear on how to use punctuation, ask a tutor or English teacher.

Many of the questions on the Writing and Language section will take a broad, editorial focus. If you have ever exchanged papers with a fellow student and given each other feedback on the placement of sentences or paragraphs and the need to add or eliminate information, you've done this kind of work. An effective piece of writing is clear, concise, and direct. That's the goal you're trying to achieve everywhere on the Writing Test, and particularly on these editorial questions.

Polish your transitions.

One type of question you can pretty much expect to see will test you on your ability to correctly use transitional words and phrases. These are single words and short phrases that take you from one thought to another, either from paragraph to paragraph or sentence to sentence.

Some transitions use a preposition. Others don't. Here are a few of the transition words you should know. There are many, many more. Transition words are effective tools to use in your SAT Essay, by the way. Take a look at the gray box to see examples of transition words and phrases that you should know how to use.

Common Transition Words and Phrases

above all	besides	in case	nonetheless	though
accordingly	but	in conclusion	on (the) condition (that)	thus
admittedly	by contrast	in contrast	on the other hand	to begin with
after (this)	consequently	in either case	on the whole	to change the topic
afterwards	conversely	in order that	only if	to conclude (with)
albeit	despite (this)	in order to	otherwise	to get back to the point
all in all	due to (the fact that)	in short	owing to (the fact)	to put it briefly
all the same	either way	in spite of (this)	provided that	to resume
altogether	even if	in summary	rather	to return to the subject
anyhow	even more	in that case	regardless (of this)	to start with
anyway	even though	in the (first, second, etc.) place	secondly	under those circumstances
as	eventually	in the end	since	unless
as a consequence	finally	in the event that	so	whatever happens
as a final point	first of all	incidentally	so as to	when in fact
as a result	for the purpose of	indeed	so that	whereas
as previously stated	granted (that)	initially	still	while
as/so long as	hence	instead	subsequently	with this in mind
at any rate	however	lastly	that being the case	yet
at first	if	more importantly	then	
at least	if not	moreover	therefore	
be that as it may	if so	nevertheless	thirdly	
because (of the fact that)	in any case	next		
before (this)	in as much as			

Here's an example that requires you to choose the correct transition:

> To American students, foreign students in their midst offer new perspectives. <u>As a result,</u> except for soccer, Europeans are not as focused on sports as the typical American can be.
>
> A) NO CHANGE
>
> B) All in all,
>
> C) However,
>
> D) For example,

Is *as a result* the strongest possible transition in that spot? The first sentence asserts that foreign students offer new perspectives. The information in the second sentence is not a result of the new perspectives offered, so *ZAP* choice A.

Choice B isn't great, but it isn't horrible either, so let's keep it around in case we don't find anything better. Choice C, *however*, is a transition that signals a contradiction. Does the second sentence contradict the first? No. *ZAP* C. How about choice D? In the first sentence, we learn that foreign students offer new perspectives. In the second sentence, we learn that Europeans aren't as focused on sports as Americans are, except for soccer. That sounds like an example of a new perspective, which makes Choice D the strongest choice for a transition like this.

To Punctuate or Not to Punctuate?

If a transition word or phrase serves as an introduction to a sentence, it's often followed by a comma. *For example,* the first two words in this sentence serve as an introduction and are followed by a comma. When the same words are used in the middle of a sentence, *instead*, the transition will often be preceded and followed by a comma. A transition used at the end of a sentence may simply be preceded by a comma, *however*.

Make sense? Give it a try. Write three sentences using transitions and punctuate them correctly.

Beginning: _____

_____

Middle: _____

_____

End: _____

_____

Match pronouns to nouns in gender and number.

The antecedent is the noun or subject to which the pronoun refers. For example, in the sentence "Joe went to the store because he needed some milk," the pronoun is *he*, and the pronoun's antecedent is *Joe*. In simple terms, *he* is *Joe*. Whenever you see a pronoun, be sure to track its antecedent—draw lines in the text from the pronoun to the noun if you need to.

The point of doing this is that the pronoun needs to match the noun it refers to both in number (one or more than one) and gender (male, female, or neutral). If it doesn't, it's wrong, and you'll need to select the answer choice that corrects it.

When the antecedent (the noun that the pronoun refers to) appears in an earlier sentence, sometimes it's difficult to keep track of the subject to which the pronoun refers. This is another case where verbalizing each sentence will help you. When you say a sentence in your head, you will often be able to hear whether or not a pronoun matches its antecedent.

Here's an example of incorrect pronoun-antecedent agreement:

> Marketing studies show that when people see an attractive person using a product, **he** identifies with the person and may consequently purchase the advertised item.

Here's the same sentence with the correct pronoun-antecedent agreement:

> Marketing studies show that when people see an attractive person using a product, **they** identify with the person and may consequently purchase the advertised item.

In relatively plain speech, the first sentence begins with *people*, a neutral-gender, plural noun, as its subject, then shifts incorrectly to *he*, a male-gender, singular noun. The second sentence is correct. *They* is a neutral, plural noun that refers to the neutral, plural word, *people*. Make sense?

Try this brief exercise in tracking a pronoun back to its antecedent.

The pronoun *it* is used several times in the following paragraph, but *it* does not refer to the same noun each time. Having too many pronouns without clear antecedents creates confusion.

> The world's population is already in excess of seven billion people, and it is expected to reach as much as 11 billion by the year 2100. It is impossible to predict how we will be able to provide food and goods for all the world's people, or how we can maintain a livable environment. <u>It</u> is not limited to third-world countries. Even the world's leading industrial nations must deal with the environmental cost of population growth and the stress that will be placed upon infrastructure by the number of vehicles those people will require.

Notice the word *it*, underlined at the beginning of the third sentence. On the Writing and Language Test, SAT will frequently underline a word or phrase and give you four options to use in that spot. Here are your options for replacing *it* in the third sentence:

A) NO CHANGE

B) The problem

C) The world's population

D) The answer

In context, which choice best clarifies what the writer is telling us about? If the underlined part is fine the way it is, your answer is A. If not, try the other choices in context and see which one makes the most sense.

Keeping A doesn't help the reader understand what *it* refers do. The sentence is still nebulous. What about B? Does it make sense to say, "*The problem* is not limited to third-world countries"? Sounds likely, so let's keep it for now. How about C? If we plug in *the world's population*, we read, "*The world's population* is not limited to third-world countries." Well, of course it's not, but that doesn't mean this statement makes sense. What about D? "The *answer* is not limited to third-world countries." That might make sense, but we'll have to read the entire paragraph to be sure. Is there anything in the paragraph that refers to *the answer*? Not really. So let's go back to B. Is there anything in the paragraph that refers to *the problem*? Absolutely. The first part of the paragraph talks about how to "provide food and goods for all the world's people" and "how we can maintain a livable environment." In addition, the last sentence talks about *the environmental cost* and *the stress* on the infrastructure, both of which are problems. The best answer is B.

Sentences run parallel just like railroad tracks.

Some sentences on the SAT will contain lists or sequences, including noun-and-verb clauses and phrases. Whenever a list is included in a sentence, each thing on the list must have the same (parallel) grammatical construction. If you master parallelism, you can turn hard questions into easy ones. If a sentence presents a sequence or list of any kind, everything listed must have parallel structure.

For example:

Set in the American Southwest, Tony Hillerman's mystery novels offer the reader details about Navajo and Hopi culture as well as <u>having suspenseful plots.</u>

A) NO CHANGE

B) have suspenseful plots.

C) they offer suspenseful plots.

D) suspenseful plots.

Choice D is correct because the author offers two things to readers, and both things need to be structured in the same way. If you simplify the sentence to its core elements, it's easy to see: *The novels offer details and plots.*

Conjunctions serve as red flags to stop and check for parallel construction.

It's especially important to track parallelism when listing prepositional phrases. A sequence of phrases must have the same basic grammatical structure. Conjunctions often hold such phrases together in a sentence. Examples include:

and   but   for   either/or   not only   but also

When you spot a conjunction, be especially alert to check for parallel construction.

For example:

Parallel Prepositional Phrase: Aretha Franklin's longevity as a successful performing artist has depended **on the superb quality** of her singing voice and **on her ability** to adapt the trends of popular music to her own creative style.

Parallel Verb Phrase: In order to prepare for the symposium, Sandy organiz**ed** the lecture, pick**ed** up the posters, and rearrang**ed** the room.

Parallelism with Correlative Conjunction: Signed into law in 1972, Title IX not only **expanded** women's opportunities in sports, but it also **made** academic gains for women possible.

Coordinating conjunctions can determine the logic of a sentence.

Coordinating conjunctions connect two parts of a sentence. They can also play a very important role in relating the logic and positive or negative tone of a sentence. Pay close attention to reversal and supporting words such as *and* and *but* that connect two parts of a sentence.

Remember, *and* is a supporting word that indicates no change in the tone of the sentence. *But* is a reversal word and, therefore, will indicate a change in tone from positive to negative or negative to positive. *So* is a cause-and-effect word that connects something that happened, is happening, or will happen as a result of that action.

For example:

Reversal: The price of petroleum products remains affordable, *but* the price does not reflect the long-term cost of depleting a non-renewable resource.

Supporting: The price of petroleum products does not reflect the long-term cost of depleting a non-renewable resource, *and* we ignore that cost at our peril.

Cause-and-effect: The price of petroleum products does not reflect the long-term cost of depleting a non-renewable resource, *so* the price remains low despite the environmental costs.

Organization, Style, and Evidence Tips

 Paragraph by paragraph, consider the organization.

One of the most important aspects of paragraph development is its organization. This is not an issue of right and wrong so much as an issue of clarity and artistry. Many well-developed paragraphs follow a general, three-part format:

Topic sentence: This sentence often comes first. It introduces the subject of the paragraph and gives the reader a hint of what will be discussed in the sentences to follow. It is the most general of the sentences listed because its purpose is simply to introduce what is to come.

Supporting sentences: These sentences will explain and illustrate the topic of the paragraph that was introduced by the topic sentence. These will be detail sentences that offer specific information.

Concluding sentence: In a free-standing paragraph, the concluding sentence will tie things up, usually by drawing a conclusion from what has been said in the paragraph's middle. In a collection of paragraphs, the conclusion often includes a transition into the upcoming paragraph.

 Watch for "command of evidence" questions.

The new test emphasizes what it calls "command of evidence." They'll ask you to demonstrate it in different ways on the reading and writing sections. On the Writing Test, that type of question may take any of several forms.

- Which choice is most effective at opening the paragraph?
- Which choice best sets up the paragraph?
- If the writer were to add a concluding sentence, which choice would best restate the main argument of the passage?
- The writer wants to add a conclusion that [accomplishes a specific purpose]. Which choice offers the best concluding sentence for that purpose?
- Which choice offers the best supporting example to strengthen the writer's argument?

Many of these questions are disguised main-idea questions. The right answer will be the best fit to the main idea expressed in the paragraph or the passage.

Don't change point of view in the middle of a passage.

Just like the old saying, "Don't change horses in the middle of a stream" (Seriously? Who would do that?), a writer shouldn't switch between points of view within a single passage. Some authors do that in their novels by alternating the point of view in chapters or sections, but it's not good practice to do it in a passage used on the SAT. If you see that, you'll know immediately that an error has to be fixed. That's right, you'll *ZAP* NO CHANGE.

In case you need a refresher, here are some quick examples to illustrate point of view. Circle the pronouns in the examples below:

> **First person:** Pancakes are my absolute favorite breakfast food! I'd eat a mile-high stack with gobs of butter and a generous coating of syrup if anyone would serve it to me. I want some now!

> **Second person:** If you want to eat a delicious breakfast, cook up a batch of pancakes. Be sure you cover them with fresh strawberries or blueberries. You'll never find a tastier treat.

> **Third person:** When someone wants to eat a breakfast that's out-of-this-world delicious, there's nothing like pancakes! He or she can make the pancakes even tastier with a generous slab of butter and a whole lot of syrup. One could never eat a tastier breakfast.

Note that the first-person example uses the personal pronouns *my*, *I*, and *me*. In this case, the writer is speaking about him- or herself. The second-person example uses the pronoun *you* to speak directly to the reader. In the third-person example, the writer is more distant from the reader, speaking about the subject *someone* with the pronouns *he*, *she*, *him*, *her*, and *one*.

You won't have to be able to name the point of view used in the SAT, but you may need to correct a sentence or paragraph that's written with mixed points of view.

Be formal or funny, but be consistent.

As you read, pay attention to the writing style. Is the writing stiff and formal? Casual but informative? Persuasive and opinionated? Or simply funny? Whatever the writing style, once you have a good feel for how the writer is trying to convey his or her message, it should be pretty easy to identify when a sentence or a word interrupts that flow with language that doesn't match.

For example, a writer who is giving a formal presentation of a serious issue probably wouldn't throw in slang for no particular reason. A writer who is trying to persuade will use specific examples and targeted language, not wishy-washy vocabulary. If you're just not sure whether a certain word or phrase fits, trust your ear; you'll probably be right.

Be ready to incorporate data into written form.

On the Writing Test, command of evidence also involves your ability to extract data from a graph, chart, or table and decide the best way to incorporate it into a passage. You will *not* have to correct punctuation, usage, or sentence structure on a chart.

These questions often look like this: A sentence or part of a sentence will be underlined. The underlined part will state a fact from the graph or chart, or offer an interpretation of some aspect of the graph or chart. The question will ask which choice states the fact or interprets the data correctly. On these questions, NO CHANGE will always be an option.

Examine the underlined bit first. If it looks right based on the graph, NO CHANGE is your answer. If it doesn't look right, check the choices for one that's better.

You might also be asked a question in this form: "The graph offers evidence that. . . ." Consider the answer choices as a series of true/false statements. Use the graph to verify each one. The one that's true is the correct answer.

Here are some sample data questions that you might encounter.

- Which choice most accurately interprets the data in the graph?
- Which of the following choices is an accurate interpretation of the data?
- Which choice offers the best summary of the data in the chart?
- The graph offers evidence that. . . .

It's important not to get bogged down with these graphics. They will not be especially complex or sophisticated, and you don't need to understand every nuance. But you do need to pay close attention to detail.

You may need to do any of the following:

- understand the main idea
- locate data points
- identify trends
- make comparisons between data or graph lines

You've done this many times before in classes such as science and history. In the Writing Test, you're not expected to understand any scientific or historical data; you're just asked to read and interpret the graphic and then choose the most accurate description among the choices. You can do that!

Chapter 3

Grammar Review

The Evidence-Based Writing Test will assess a variety of skills, including some fairly picky grammatical concepts. Since you probably haven't seen some of these rules in print since grade school or middle school, use the following Grammar Review section to refresh your memory.

Common Punctuation Mistakes

When you send texts and emails, do you tend to ignore most of the punctuation rules your English teachers taught you? Most people do. But the PSAT and SAT require you to understand and correctly use punctuation. There are no shortcuts allowed. So let's review the most common rules.

Periods

A period ends a complete sentence. A complete sentence contains both a *subject* (who or what is doing the action) and a *predicate* (the action). If one of these is missing, you have a *sentence fragment*.

The moldy sandwich, a fuzzy-green and smelly entity.

> There is no predicate. What is the moldy sandwich *doing*?

Lives in the fridge and continues to grow.

> There is no subject. We don't know *what* "lives in the fridge and continues to grow."

 The moldy sandwich, a fuzzy-green and smelly entity, lives in the fridge and continues to grow.

> The sentence has both subject and predicate. We know what's doing the action ("the moldy sandwich"), and we know what the action is ("lives . . . and continues to grow").

Commas

A comma is simply a signal to the reader to pause. There are many rules for the use of commas, but most situations are covered by the following "Fab Four" comma rules:

1. **After items in a series**: If you list three or more items in a row, place a comma after each item in the series except the last one.

 John, Paul, George, and Ringo first recorded together in 1962.

It's also perfectly acceptable to omit the comma between the last two items in a series. Whether or not you choose to add the serial comma, the important thing is to be consistent. Whether or not to use a serial comma won't be tested on the SAT or PSAT; it's an editorial choice.

 John, Paul, George and Ringo first recorded together in 1962.

2. **After an introductory phrase:** An introductory phrase is a short phrase at the beginning of a sentence that introduces the main idea of the sentence. An introductory phrase is followed by a comma.

 By the end of 1964, the Beatles had several number-one records in England.

 Though it may not have seemed overly important at the time, the "British Invasion" marked the beginning of a new era in rock 'n' roll history.

3. **To set off information that's not essential to the meaning of the sentence:**

   • A *parenthetical expression* is a phrase that modifies the entire sentence. Common parenthetical expressions include: *as a matter of fact*, *believe me*, *I am sure*, *to tell the truth*, and *it seems to me*. Parenthetical expressions need to be set off by commas.

 The Beatles' most experimental album, in my opinion, is *Sgt. Pepper's Lonely Hearts Club Band.*

A parenthetical expression is not necessary to the meaning of the sentence; it's almost like an aside. As a matter of fact, you could remove it altogether and the sentence would still be acceptable.

 The Beatles' most experimental album is *Sgt. Pepper's Lonely Hearts Club Band.*

   • An *appositive* is a group of words that describes a noun or a pronoun. Appositives can appear at the beginning, middle, or end of a sentence. An appositive is set off by commas.

 Paul McCartney, perhaps the most musically proficient of the Fab Four, played bass guitar.

Like a parenthetical expression, an appositive is not essential to the meaning of the sentence. What would happen if we just took it out?

Paul McCartney played bass guitar.

The sentence would still be acceptable.

Here are some additional examples:

The Beatle, who played the drums, was the last to join the group.

The words *who played the drums* are necessary for the reader to know which Beatle is being discussed; *do not* set the phrase off with commas.

Now look at the next sentence:

Ringo, who played the drums, was the last to join the group.

Here, the phrase *who played the drums* is *not* essential information; we have all the information we need with Ringo's name. Set it off with commas.

The album, recorded just before the band's breakup, was *Abbey Road*.

The words r*ecorded just before the band's breakup* are necessary for the reader to know which album is being talked about; *do not* set them off with commas.

4. **To separate independent clauses**: An independent clause is a string of words that can stand alone as a sentence; it contains both a subject and a predicate. When two independent clauses are joined by a comma and a conjunction (*and, but, or, nor, for*), you have a *compound sentence*.

John, Paul, and George all played guitar, Ringo played the drums.

This sentence needs a conjunction.

John, Paul, and George all played guitar but Ringo played the drums.

This sentence needs a comma.

John, Paul, and George all played guitar, but Ringo played the drums.

This sentence has both a comma and a conjunction.

Write a sentence using a comma(s) correctly:

_____

_____

_____

Semicolons

Semicolons are also used to link independent clauses, but *without* the use of a conjunction. A semicolon acts much like a period; everything on both sides of the semicolon must be able to stand alone as a sentence. A semicolon links two ideas more closely than a period does.

 LaMarcus Aldridge is a powerful player; his size and strength make him a formidable obstacle on the court.

Everything on both sides of the semicolon can stand alone as a sentence.

LaMarcus Aldridge is a powerful player; and his size and strength make him a formidable obstacle on the court.

No conjunction is needed.

A semicolon also separates items in a list, much like a comma does. Use semicolons to make a list less confusing when there are already commas separating things within the list.

 Please find the following items for the party: a CD player; a birthday cake, but not the kind with icky-sweet icing; a location that has a kitchen, folding tables, chairs, and air conditioning; and plenty of invitations.

A semicolon is never interchangeable with a colon or a dash.

Write a sentence using a semicolon correctly:

_____

_____

_____

Colons

A colon causes a break in a sentence and calls the reader's attention to what follows. Use a colon in the following ways:

1. To explain or add emphasis to the first clause in a sentence:

 David Letterman did something no other late-night talk show host had done: He hired his own mom as a correspondent.

> Did you notice that the second clause started with a capital letter? Here's an example where there's more than one way to write a sentence correctly. An independent clause following a colon can either start with a capital or, like the sentence below, it can begin with a lowercase letter. Either is correct. Don't worry, you won't be offered the choice between two correct—but different—sentences.

 David Letterman did something no other late-night talk show host had done: he hired his own mom as a correspondent.

2. To introduce a list following an independent clause:

 I have three simple wishes for my birthday: a year's supply of iTunes, a summer vacation in Europe, and a guest appearance on *Dancing with the Stars*.

3. To introduce a quotation that relates strongly to the clause before it:

 In the midst of her most pressing problems, she comforted herself with a saying she'd heard since childhood: "This is a job for Kool-Aid!"

Write a sentence using a colon correctly:

_____

_____

_____

Dashes

Dashes are used to set off information that is not necessary to the meaning of the sentence, somewhat like commas do.

The Woodstock II concert—a pale imitation of the original—was an overpriced fiasco.

Today I went to Britches-R-Us—the one in the mall next to the music store—to shop for a new pair of jeans and a belt.

Dashes are also used to emphasize sentence elements.

A new scientific study has indicated a characteristic consistent in highly successful people—a love of chocolate.

Write a sentence using dashes correctly:

_____

_____

Apostrophes

An apostrophe indicates possession. The apostrophe comes before the *s* when the noun is singular and after the *s* when the noun is plural.

Dave's mom   **Spike's camera**

the girls' books   **the doctors' opinions**

The possessive can also be stated as follows (though it's pretty clunky sounding):

the mother of Dave

but never:

the mother of Dave's

However, when a plural noun does not already end in *s*, add an apostrophe + *s*.

the children's toys

the mice's cheese

With indefinite pronouns, the apostrophe always comes before the *s*.

<u>Everyone's</u> expectation was that the team would eventually return to the state finals. Whether the team actually would was <u>anyone's</u> guess.

Write a sentence using an apostrophe correctly:

_____

_____

Parentheses

Parentheses are used to set off information that is not essential to the meaning of the sentence.

 Who would have thought that Superman (he calls himself the "Man of Steel") would wear tights made by his mom?

What's the difference between commas, dashes, and parentheses?

Not much. When you want to set off information that is not essential to the meaning of the sentence, whether you use commas, dashes, or parentheses is often an editorial choice. The editors will not ask you to make arbitrary decisions.

They _will_, however, ask you to be consistent, at least within the same sentence. The sentences below are all acceptable.

 Students often differ from their parents and teachers, and among themselves, on many issues.

 Students often differ from their parents and teachers—and among themselves—on many issues.

 Students often differ from their parents and teachers (and among themselves) on many issues.

Inconsistent punctuation in the following sentences makes them unacceptable.

Students often differ from their parents and teachers—and among themselves, on many issues.

Students often differ from their parents and teachers, and among themselves—on many issues.

Don't mismatch them!

Write a sentence using parentheses correctly:

_____

_____

Common Usage Mistakes

What's wrong with this sentence?

Everyone here should have their books.

It sounds okay to most people, but in formal speech and in writing it is more acceptable to say:

Everyone here should have <u>his</u> book.

Since many people prefer to avoid the generic pronoun *he* when talking about a male or female, *his or her* is commonly used:

Everyone here should have <u>his or her</u> book.

Of course, if you know the gender of the person, you would say so:

Somebody on the girls' basketball team forgot <u>her</u> gym bag.

Watch for pronouns on the Writing Test. Whenever a pronoun is underlined, quickly check for its antecedent (what it is referring to).

The possibilities for interacting with art, rather than gazing mutely at <u>them</u>, are endless.

In the previous sentence, *them* refers to *art* and should be changed to *it*.

Other cases of pronoun-antecedent agreement are more subtle:

The team pays <u>their</u> own travel expenses.

Team is a collective noun, requiring a singular verb (*pays*) and a singular pronoun. Hence, *their* should be changed to *its*.

The team members pay <u>their</u> own travel expenses.

In the sentence above, *their* refers to *members*, a plural noun. This is correct.

The following pronouns require singular verbs and antecedents:

anybody, anyone, each, either, everybody, everyone, everything, neither, nobody, no one, one, somebody, someone, something

The following pronouns always take a plural verb and antecedent:

both, many, several, all

These pronouns can be plural or singular, depending on how they are used:

all, any, none, some

For example:

All *of you are* fine students.   Plural—"All of you"

All *of my dinner is* ruined.   Singular—"All of my dinner"

It is easy to become confused when choosing between singular and plural forms. That's why you're likely to see a few agreement questions on the Writing Test. Here are two other ways that the Writing Test makes it hard to know whether to use a singular or plural verb:

1. **Fake compound subject:**

   The list of repairs and hours of labor <u>is/are</u> too large.

   It sounds like the list of repairs and the hours of labor are both too large.

   The only thing that is too large is the list, which happens to contain repairs and hours of labor. You wouldn't say that the hours of labor are too large, so you could tell that *list* is the subject. The correct verb would be *is*.

2. **Reversed order of subject and verb:**

   What is the subject in this sentence?

   In the middle of the park <u>stand/stands</u> two fine statues.

   Statues is the subject, so the verb should be *stand*: **Two fine statues stand in the park.**

   Be extra careful when the normal order of the sentence is reversed.

Regular Verbs

A regular verb is one that forms its past and past participle by adding *-ed* or *-d* to the infinitive form.

Infinitive	Past	Past Participle
dance	danced	(have) danced
kick	kicked	(have) kicked
play	played	(have) played

Irregular Verbs

An irregular verb is one that forms its past and past participle in some way other than a regular verb. Some irregular verbs form the past and past participle forms by changing the vowels, some by changing the consonants, and others by making no change at all. The following is a list of common irregular verbs:

Infinitive	Past	Past Participle
begin	began	(have) begun
blow	blew	(have) blown
break	broke	(have) broken
bring	brought	(have) brought
burst	burst	(have) burst
choose	chose	(have) chosen
come	came	(have) come
do	did	(have) done
drink	drank	(have) drunk
drive	drove	(have) driven
fall	fell	(have) fallen
freeze	froze	(have) frozen
give	gave	(have) given
go	went	(have) gone
ride	rode	(have) ridden
ring	rang	(have) rung
run	ran	(have) run
see	saw	(have) seen
shrink	shrank	(have) shrunk
speak	spoke	(have) spoken
steal	stole	(have) stolen
swim	swam	(have) swum
take	took	(have) taken
throw	threw	(have) thrown
write	wrote	(have) written

Chapter 4

The SAT Essay

You will *not* be required to write an essay when you take the PSAT. However, if you go on to take the SAT, you may want to do so. For that reason, it is important to know what this section of the test is about.

For several years, the SAT essay was required for all students taking the test. The new SAT makes writing the essay optional—however, the choice to take it does not lie with students. *Colleges* have already made that decision and can require incoming students to submit an SAT essay score, or they may have decided this part of the test is not necessary. Colleges requiring the essay in the past are likely to continue to require it; that includes many of the most selective schools in the United States.

Many students have particular colleges in mind before they take the SAT. If the schools they're interested in don't require a score from the essay portion, the students don't register for or take it. This is risky. If you don't take the essay part of the test and decide later to apply to a college that does require it, you will need to take the entire SAT again just to get the essay score. For that reason, we recommend that you register for the entire test and take the essay portion along with the other sections on test day. If colleges you are interested in don't require it, you will still have a score on file. If your college plans change and you end up applying to a school where the essay section is required, you will have a score to submit.

Prompt	Time	PSAT	SAT
1	50 minutes	N/A	Optional

What to Expect

The SAT essay is designed to show your reading comprehension, your analytical reasoning, and your writing skills. You'll read a nonfiction passage ranging between 650 and 750 words. In the passage, an author will make one or more arguments—state a claim. Your assignment will be to write an essay that explains how the author builds that main argument in the passage. You will have 50 minutes to read the passage, plan your essay, and write it.

In the past, essays were scored holistically, meaning the entire essay was assessed for good, coherent writing that was on topic and responded well to the prompt. Essays are looked at in a more involved way now. A 2-to-8 scale is used so that three traits are assessed:

- **Reading:** how well the essay you wrote demonstrates your understanding of the passage you read
- **Analysis:** how well you understood the task and evaluated the author's reasoning, as well as the quality of your own reasoning
- **Writing:** how well you communicated your ideas in terms of organization, sentence structure, word choice, style, tone, and conventions

The essay score will be reported separately from the scores you receive for Evidence-Based Reading and Writing and for Math.

Essay Tips

Read *all* of the instructions before you read the passage.

The essay assignment has three parts: the instructions for reading the passage, the passage itself, and the instructions for writing. The essay will be easier to write if you read *all* of the instructions before you start reading the passage. So start with the instructions for reading, skip over the passage itself, and then read the instructions for writing.

The instructions for reading the passage will look something like this:

As you read the passage below, consider how the author uses

- evidence, which may include examples and facts, to support his or her arguments
- reasoning to expand ideas and to connect arguments and their support
- elements of writing, which could include word choice and appeals to readers' emotion, as well as other persuasive techniques to strengthen his or her ideas

The instructions for writing will read very much like the following paragraphs. The underlined portion will change depending on the content of the passage you're given, but the rest of the assignment will be the same. Read very carefully so you understand exactly what you're expected to do.

Write an essay in which you explain how the author builds an argument that <u>the rise of social media has increased political polarization in America</u>. In your essay, analyze how the author uses one or more of the features listed in the directions to persuade readers that there is more to consider than the figures the public is handed. Be sure your analysis focuses on the most significant parts of the passage.

Your essay should not explain how you feel about the topic or this situation. It should tell how the author works to persuade his or her reading audience.

By prereading the instructions, you will know in advance what your written analysis has to be about—in this case, how the author builds an argument that the rise of social media has increased political polarization in America. As you read the passage, you can be on the lookout for specific elements pertaining to that instruction. If you wait until after you've read the passage to find out what you will be writing about, you will waste time rereading to hunt for pertinent elements.

As you read the passage, consider evidence, reasoning, and style, and decide why the author wrote the piece.

This is specifically what those first Big Three are all about:

Evidence includes the facts and examples the author uses in support of the claims he or she makes. In many passages, the author will make a statement in the first paragraph that steers the rest of the text. Think about the factual information and point of view the author presents. Look for reputable sources cited along with factual information. Find where he uses relevant examples to back up his claim. It is often helpful to underline this information as you come across it when reading the text.

Reasoning pertains to the development of ideas, as well as the connection of claims to evidence. Pay attention to how the author builds her case. It may be subtle, asking readers to make inferences based on evidence she is citing. It may be obvious: statistics and facts are mentioned specifically to back up her claim. Decide whether the author's ideas are developed logically or if you are being asked to take her word for it, without solid information to back it up.

Stylistic or persuasive elements involves the effectiveness of structure and language. Some writers may provide an anecdote at the start of their passage as a way to set the tone. Others may appeal to readers in emotional or logical ways. Word choice is important. Think about how she uses certain words or phrases to back up her claim and to make readers feel a certain way about the topic.

So stick to the Big Three basics with one exception…

Consider the author's purpose.

One key to analyzing any text is to understand **the author's purpose**. What is the author trying to accomplish? What does the author want you to think, do, and/ or feel? The author's purpose shapes all of the choices he or she makes in terms of claims, evidence, and style.

As you read, consider the overall purpose of the text. With that in mind, it will be easier to make judgments about evidence, reasoning, and style.

Do NOT use "features of your own choice."

The instructions for reading say you should use the author's evidence, reasoning, and stylistic or persuasive elements within your analysis of the passage. It also suggests "features of your own choice" as valid in your analysis of the passage.

Evidence, reasoning, and stylistic or persuasive elements will be the most important features of the passage by far. Any others you try to identify and use will be trivial in comparison, and scorers won't be impressed. You almost certainly won't raise your score by mentioning additional features within the passage.

Keep in mind that you only have 50 minutes for the essay. Unless a startling insight hits you like a flash of lightning, don't waste your precious minutes looking for a novel idea or approach to writing the essay. Instead, use all the time you have to plan and write a coherent, cohesive—and solid—essay.

Make notes as you read.

It's vital to keep your pencil active as you read the passage, or else you'll find yourself hopelessly lost when it's time to write. As briefly mentioned above, underline, circle, and/or draw boxes around parts of the text you can use as you write your essay. One good way to do it is in this format:

- Circle claims made by the author
- Underline facts intended to support claims, such as statistics or quotations from experts
- Box words and sentences intended to appeal to emotions

By marking claims, facts, and stylistic or persuasive elements in this way, you will have identified the most significant parts of the passage, which are the ones you need to use to write your analysis.

Make notes in the margins to elaborate on your markings. Specify what emotions certain language evokes in you. If a claim or fact sparks a question in your mind, jot it down. In fact, make a note of anything that comes to mind while you're reading. You're collecting raw material for the essay you will write. Get it all down. You can decide later what to use and what to ignore. Remember that the essay scorers won't be looking at any of your notes. Be sure to include all important ideas within your written essay response.

The essay is not about you.

The last part of the SAT writing assignment makes it very clear what your essay should *not* be about. Reread those two sentences now:

Your essay should not explain whether you agree with the author's claims. It should explain how the author builds an argument to persuade the audience.

You may feel strongly that the rise of social media has indeed contributed to political polarization in America, but your personal opinion is *irrelevant* to this assignment. It is also not important that you keep getting political emails and you're not of voting age. None of that kind of personal information is included in this type of essay. Instead, you are directed to analyze the way the author makes the argument specified in the assignment. That's all. If you express your own feelings about it, or do anything other than directly address the ways in which the author builds the argument he or she is making, it will affect your score—and not in a good way, no matter how passionate or eloquent you are.

Budget your time by using Ready-Set-Go.

You will have 50 minutes to read the passage and write your essay. Monitor the time carefully as you work by using what we call *Ready-Set-Go.*

- **Ready:** Allow yourself about 15 minutes to read the directions at the top of the passage, below the passage (the analysis prompt), and then the passage itself. You don't need to do more than just skim the general directions before the passage, as you will already know what to do by practicing with the prompts in your Study Guide. What you want to pay close attention to is the specific directions that come below the passage. These tell you exactly what you are expected to do. As you are reading, make notes on the page.

- **Set:** Allow approximately 10 minutes to plan and organize your essay.

- **Go:** Take the bulk of the remaining time (25–30 minutes) to write the essay. Plan to devote part of that time to re-reading your finished essay to make sure your analysis will be clear to anyone who reads it. (You know what you meant to say. But will it be clear to somebody else?) Be sure to proofread your essay, too, so you can correct errors in punctuation, grammar, or spelling.

Use what you already know about the structure of a good essay.

By the time you take the SAT, you have probably done a great deal of academic writing, especially if you are taking Advanced Placement courses or doing other kinds of advanced work in school. The same skills that have led you to succeed on these assignments will lead you to success on the SAT essay. Here is the best way to structure your essay:

- Use the first paragraph to make a clear and specific claim about how the author builds his or her argument.
- Support your claim with relevant and specific evidence *taken from the passage* (this is not the time to be making things up or drawing from your own experience).
- Use precise language and an appropriate tone for academic writing.
- Vary your sentence structure.
- Pay close attention to grammar, punctuation, and spelling.
- Write a conclusion that ties up what you have said in your essay.

Practice writing an essay before the actual SAT.

Use the sample prompts to write your own essay and take it under test conditions. That means sitting at a table with just a sheet of paper, a watch or timer, and a pencil. Read the instructions and the passage, make notes, then plan and write an essay within a 50-minute time frame.

Random DOs and DON'Ts

- **Do** write neatly. Scorers can only rate your work based on what they are able to read. Ensure your writing is legible—use cursive or printing, whichever you do better. Either is acceptable as long as your essay can be read.
- **Don't** write extra-large just to fill up the page. The scorers won't be fooled.
- **Don't** draw pictures, write commentary, or add anything to your essay that is not directly related to your assignment.
- **Do** transition well from one paragraph to another. That's smooth writing. Refer to the list of transition words and phrases included on page 23 in this Study Guide.
- **Do** create a response that covers as much of the available space as you can. Make your analysis strong by using as many important details from the text as you are able. A short essay, even if well constructed, won't be likely to earn the maximum score.
- **Do** reread your work slowly and carefully in the final minutes of the allotted time. Insert clear, common proofreading marks if you don't have time to actually erase and change any part of your essay. Circling a misspelled word, for example, and writing its correct spelling in the margin could be a better choice than just leaving it spelled incorrectly.

Scoring

Two scorers independently score each essay. These scorers will each award a point value from 4 (the highest) to 1 to show the essay writer's proficiency in three areas: how closely the writer read the text, how well the writer analyzed it, and the writer's skill level.

The score points will be totaled, for a maximum score of 24 (essays receiving a 4 in each category and from both scorers) and a minimum of 6 (essays receiving a 1 in each category from both scorers).

Here is how each point value is generally assessed:

Points	Reading	Analysis	Writing
4 This essay score is given to show advanced work.	The essay demonstrates in-depth understanding of the text, its main idea, and how the important details work together for a cohesive piece of writing. The student's essay demonstrates comprehension by being free from factual errors and misinterpretations of the text. It uses quoted or paraphrased evidence from the source document to prove comprehension of the material.	The essay offers a strong analysis with clear insight into the text. The student shows a level of complexity with regard to the text analysis. The response shows a well organized and thoughtful discussion of ideas in the text, and includes appropriate and significant support for these ideas. The response stays on topic and considers parts of the text that directly apply to the claim and supporting this claim.	This essay demonstrates a clear understanding of the use of standard written English. The essay includes a cohesively written central claim, introduction, excellent progression of ideas, and a strong conclusion. The essay flows well, with deliberate strong word choice, impartial tone, and proper appropriate style. The response is free from errors or contains very few, and demonstrates a strong command of the conventions of standard written English.
3 This essay score is given to show proficient work.	The essay demonstrates a proficient understanding of the text, its main idea, and how the important details work together for a cohesive piece of writing. The student's essay demonstrates comprehension by being generally free from factual errors regarding the text, and it uses evidence from the source document to prove comprehension of the material.	The response provides a generally effective analysis with insight into the text. The student displays adequate complexity with regard to the text analysis. The response shows a skilled discussion of ideas in the text, and includes some appropriate and significant support for these ideas. The response generally stays on topic and considers parts of the text that directly apply to the claim and supporting this claim.	This essay shows effective use and control of written English. The essay includes a central claim, introduction, good progression of ideas, and an adequate conclusion. The essay flows well in most spots, with good word choice, mainly impartial tone, and proper appropriate style. The response is not free from errors and demonstrates a proficient command of the conventions of standard written English.

Points	Reading	Analysis	Writing
2 This essay score is given to show partial understanding of the source text.	The essay somewhat demonstrates understanding of the text, its main idea, and how the important details work together for a cohesive piece of writing. The student's essay at least partially demonstrates comprehension but has some factual errors regarding the text, and it may not use relevant evidence from the source document to prove comprehension of the material.	The response provides a partially effective analysis displaying some insight into the text. The essay displays a basic level of understanding with regard to the text analysis. The response shows a somewhat adequate discussion of ideas in the text, although it may lack support for these ideas. The response may not always stay on topic and may consider parts of the text that do not directly apply to and support the claim.	This essay shows limited structure and skill in the conventions of standard written English. The essay includes a central claim, one or two relevant ideas, and an attempt at a conclusion but is lacking true cohesiveness. It may be missing an introduction or have an introduction that is functional but not well constructed. The essay flows adequately in most spots, with adequate word choice, but may not have a sufficiently impartial tone. The essay is functional, but has little evidence of style. The response contains errors and does not demonstrate an overall proficienct command of the conventions of standard written English.
1 This essay score is given to show inadequate work.	The essay does not demonstrate an understanding of the text, its main idea, and how the important details work together for a cohesive piece of writing. The student's essay may not show comprehension and is likely to contain factual errors regarding the text. It does use relevant evidence from the source document to prove comprehension of the material.	The response does not provide an effective analysis with insight into the text. The student fails to display an understanding of the passage within the text analysis. The response does not provide a discussion of ideas in the text, and lacks support for ideas that are included. The response may not stay on topic.	This essay shows little or no structure and skill in the conventions of standard written English. The essay may not include a central claim, introduction, progression of ideas, and/or conclusion. The essay flows unevenly, with weak word choice, uneven tone, and may lack appropriate style. The response contains errors that affect the essay's meaning and does not demonstrate an adequate command of the conventions of standard written English.

Sample Prompts

Sample Prompt #1

As you read the passage below, consider how Lord Macaulay uses

- evidence, which may include examples and facts, to support his arguments
- reasoning to expand ideas and to connect arguments and their support
- elements of writing, which could include word choice, appeals to the readers' emotions, and other persuasive techniques to strengthen his ideas

Adapted from *History of England, Volume I,* **"Introduction," 1908, by Lord Macaulay. Public domain.**

1   I propose to write the history of England from the accession of King James the Second down to a time, which is within the memory of men still living. I shall recount the errors which, in a few months, alienated a loyal gentry and priesthood from the House of Stuart. I shall trace the course of that revolution which terminated the long struggle between our sovereigns and their parliaments, and bound up together the rights of the people and the title of the reigning dynasty.

2   I shall relate how the new settlement was, during many troubled years, successfully defended against foreign and domestic enemies; how, under that settlement, the authority of law and the security of property were found to be compatible with a liberty of discussion and of individual action never before known; how, from the auspicious union of order and freedom, sprang a prosperity of which the annals of human affairs had furnished no example; how our country, from a state of ignominious vassalage, rapidly rose to the place of umpire among European powers; how her opulence and her martial glory grew together; how, by wise and resolute good faith, was gradually established a public credit fruitful of marvels which to the statesmen of any former age would have seemed incredible; how a gigantic commerce gave birth to a maritime power, compared with which every other maritime power, ancient or modern, sinks into insignificance; how Scotland, after ages of enmity, was at length united to England, not merely by legal bonds, but by indissoluble ties of interest and affection; how, in America, the British colonies rapidly became far mightier and wealthier than the realms which Cortes and Pizarro had added to the dominions of Charles the Fifth; how in Asia, British adventurers founded an empire not less splendid and more durable than that of Alexander.

3   Nor will it be less my duty faithfully to record disasters mingled with triumphs, and great national crimes and follies far more humiliating than any disaster. It will be seen that even what we justly account our chief blessings were not without alloy. It will be seen that the system which effectually secured our liberties against the encroachments of kingly power gave birth to a new class of abuses from which absolute monarchies are exempt. It will be seen that, in consequence partly of unwise interference, and partly of unwise neglect, the increase of wealth and the extension of trade produced, together with immense good, some evils from which poor and rude societies are free.

4   It will be seen how, in two important dependencies of the crown, wrong was followed by just retribution; how imprudence and obstinacy broke the ties which bound the North American colonies to the parent state; how Ireland, cursed by the domination of race over race, and of religion over religions, remained indeed a member of the empire, but a withered and distorted member, adding no strength to the body politic, and reproachfully pointed at by all who feared or envied the greatness of England.

5   Yet, unless I greatly deceive myself, the general effect of this checkered narrative will be to excite thankfulness in all religious minds, and hope in the breast of all patriots. For the history of our country during the last hundred and sixty years is eminently the history of physical, of moral, and of intellectual improvement. Those who compare the age on which their lot has fallen with a golden age which exists only in their imagination may talk of degeneracy and decay: but no man who is correctly informed as to the past will be disposed to take a morose or desponding view of the present.

Write an essay in which you explain how Lord Macaulay builds an argument to persuade his readers that England has become one of the greatest nations in history. In your essay, analyze how Macaulay uses one or more of the features listed in the directions to provide strength to his argument through logic and persuasion. Be sure your analysis focuses on the most significant parts of the passage.

Your essay should not explain how you feel about England, the British monarchy, or the British Commonwealth. It should tell how Lord Macaulay works to persuade his reading audience.

Sample Prompt #2

As you read the passage below, consider how William Douglas Morrison uses
- evidence, which may include examples and facts, to support his arguments
- reasoning to expand ideas and to connect arguments and their support
- elements of writing, which could include word choice, appeals to the readers' emotions, and other persuasive techniques to strengthen his ideas

Adapted from *Crime and Its Causes*, 1908, by William Douglas Morrison. Public domain.

1　Chapter 1: The Statistics of Crime

2　It is only within the present century, and in some countries it is only within the present generation, that the possibility has arisen of conducting the study of criminal problems on anything approaching an exact and scientific basis. Before the introduction of a system of criminal statistics—a step taken by most people within the memory of men still living—it was impossible for civilized communities to ascertain with absolute accuracy whether crime was increasing or decreasing, or what transformation it was passing through in consequence of the social, political, and economic changes constantly taking place in all highly organized societies. It was also equally impossible to appreciate the effect of punishment for good or evil on the criminal population.

3　Justice had little or no data to go upon; prisoners were sentenced in batches to the gallows, to transportation, to the hulks, or to the county jail, but no inquiry was made as to the result of these punishments on the criminal classes or on the progress of crime. It was deemed sufficient to catch and punish the offender; the more offences seemed to increase—there was no sure method of knowing whether they did increase or not—the more severe the punishment became. Justice worked in the dark, and was surrounded by the terrors of darkness. What followed is easy to imagine; the criminal law of England reached a pitch of unparalleled barbarity, and within living memory laws were on the statute book by which a man might be hanged for stealing property above the value of a shilling.

4　Had a fairly accurate system of criminal statistics existed, it is very likely that the data contained in them would have reassured the nation and tempered the severity of the law.

5　Of criminal statistics it may be said in the first place, that they act as an annual register for tabulating the amount of danger to which society is exposed by the nefarious operations of lawless persons. By these statistics we are informed of the number of crimes committed during the course of the year so far as they are reported to the police. We are informed of the number of persons brought to trial for the perpetration of these crimes; of the nature of the offenses with which incriminated persons are charged, and of the length of sentence imposed on those who are sent to prison. The age, the degree of instruction, and the occupations of prisoners are also tabulated. A record is also kept of the number of times a man has been committed to prison, and of the manner in which he has conducted himself while in confinement.

6 One important point must be mentioned on which criminal statistics are almost entirely silent. The great sources of crime are the personal, the social, and the economic conditions of the individuals who commit it. Criminal statistics, to be exhaustive, ought to include not only the amount of crime and the degrees of punishment awarded to offenders; these statistics should also, as far as practicable, take cognizance of the sources from which crime undoubtedly springs.

7 In this respect, our information, so far as it comes to us through ordinary channels, is lamentably deficient. It is confined to data respecting the age, sex, and occupation of the offender. These [pieces of] data are very interesting, and very useful, as affording a glimpse of the sources from which the dark river of delinquency takes its rise. But they are too meager and fragmentary. They require to be completed by the personal and social history of the criminal.

8 Crime is not necessarily a disease, but it resembles disease in this respect, that it will be impossible to wipe it out till an accurate diagnosis has been made of the causes which produce it. To punish crime is all very well; but punishment is not an absolute remedy; its deterrent action is limited, and other methods besides punishment must be adopted if society wishes to gain the mastery over the criminal population. What those methods should be can only be ascertained after the most searching preliminary inquiries into the main factors of crime.

9 It ought, therefore, to be a weighty part of the business of criminal statistics to offer as full information as possible, not only respecting crimes and punishments, but much more respecting criminals. Every criminal has a life history; that history is very frequently the explanation of his sinister career; it ought, therefore, to be tabulated, so that it may be seen how far his descent and his surroundings have contributed to make him what he is.

Write an essay in which you explain how William Douglas Morrison builds an argument to persuade his audience that reporting of criminal activity may not be complete. In your essay, analyze how Morrison uses one or more of the features listed in the directions to persuade readers that there is more to consider than the figures the public is provided. Be sure your analysis focuses on the most significant parts of the passage.

Your essay should not explain how you feel about criminal activity or those who commit crime. It should tell how William Douglas Morrison works to persuade his reading audience.

Chapter 5

The Math Test

The PSAT and SAT Math Tests are each divided into two major sections.

Test	Total Time/Items	Calculator-Permitted	No Calculator
PSAT	48 Items/70 minutes	31 Items/45 minutes	17 Items/25 minutes
SAT	58 Items/80 minutes	38 Items/55 minutes	20 Items/25 minutes

WAIT A MINUTE . . . THERE'S A NO-CALCULATOR SECTION??!?!!!??

Yes, but don't panic. A calculator is only a time-saver. It doesn't magically provide math knowledge you don't already possess. Even the problems in the calculator section can be done without one, though a calculator will definitely save you time.

Some of the problems in each section will not offer you choices. They will require you to come up with the answer on your own and put the answer onto a grid that can be scored by machine. For some students it's more challenging to fill in the grid properly than to actually do the math, so we'll provide some tips for doing that later in this section.

What to Expect

The PSAT and SAT divide the math content into four categories:

- Heart of Algebra
- Problem Solving and Data Analysis
- Passport to Advanced Math
- Additional Topics in Math

Heart of Algebra includes problems involving equations, systems of equations, expressions, and inequalities. **Problem Solving and Data Analysis** requires you to do problems involving ratios, percents, and proportions. You also will have to describe the relationships you see in one or more graphics and answer questions about data displayed in graphs, charts, and tables.

Passport to Advanced Math involves quadratic and other higher-order equations. You will also have to rewrite expressions and manipulate polynomials on these questions, which will make up about a quarter of the total test. **Additional Topics in Math** covers trigonometry and geometry. Only about 10 percent of the test will be devoted to this category.

The test places a heavier emphasis on Heart of Algebra and Problem Solving and Data Analysis than on Passport to Advanced Math and Additional Topics in Math. Problems from Heart of Algebra and Problem Solving and Data Analysis will make up almost two-thirds of the test.

What all this means is that the PSAT/SAT Math Test is heavily skewed toward algebra and much less interested in geometry and trig. That might be good news for some students and bad news for others.

The College Board says that the PSAT and SAT math tests are intended to reflect what students are doing in high school now and what they will be expected to do during their first year in college.

So as you approach the test, it's important to keep in mind that the skills you use in your everyday math classes are the ones you need for this test. You don't need any special, super-secret knowledge.

PSAT and SAT stress real-world applications on the test. You'll see a lot of problems that present you with real-life data of the kind you would expect to see in a science or social studies class. It might be displayed in table form, in a bar graph, a line graph, a pie chart, or some other graphic. But remember: this is a *math* test, not a science or social studies test. Try to make sense of the information, but only as much as necessary to help pull the math out of the problem. Don't worry if you don't fully understand the context provided for the information. Focus on understanding the math that the problem is asking you to do.

Math Strategy Tips

tip 1   Take Control of the Math Test.

The first step in taking control of the SAT Math sections is to shorten them up to fit your personal situation. It makes no difference if you score your points on the calculator section or the no-calculator section. On either section, a point is a point.

If your starting score is around 400, don't fantasize about moving up to a 600. Instead, think in terms of 20–30 points at a time. The number of problems you need to work and double-check depends on your target score. The following table shows what you need to do to hit various target levels.

Note: GR refers to gridded-response and MC refers to multiple-choice.

Reasonable Target SAT Math Score	To take control of the SAT Math Test, you need to be . . .
700–730	correct on 11 GR problems and 39 MC problems. Blind guess on the remaining 6 MC problems.
630–650	correct on 9 GR problems and 31 MC problems. Blind guess on the remaining 14 MC problems.
560–580	correct on 7 GR problems and 23 MC problems. Blind guess on the remaining 22 MC problems.
500–520	correct on 4 GR problems and 16 MC problems. Blind guess on the remaining 29 MC problems.
430–450	correct on 2 GR problems and 8 MC problems. Blind guess on the remaining 37 MC problems.
380–410	correct on 1 GR problems and 4 MC problems. Blind guess on the remaining 41 MC problems.

For example, if your reasonable target is an SAT Math score of 510, you need to use as much time as necessary to work and double check 4 of the 13 gridded-response problems and 16 of the multiple-choice problems—even if it takes nearly all of your test time. In the remaining minutes of each part of the test, blind guess on the other 29 multiple-choice problems. On average, you'll pick the right answer about seven times out of 29 blind guesses. Your raw score will be about 27, and your SAT score will be around 510.

The key to making this system work is to be perfect on the number of problems that you work and double-check. Careless mistakes can ruin your SAT math score.

Make three passes through the Math Test.

First Pass

- Go from item 1 through item 20 (no-calculator test) or from 1 through 38 (calculator-permitted test), working only the problems you can do quickly and easily.

- Let nothing slow you down—skip any time-consuming problems.

- Aim for 100% correct on First Pass items.

- Be extremely careful—don't make stupid mistakes.

Second Pass

- Go back to the beginning and start over.

- Work the harder items that you know how to work.

- Skip or guess at the demons—the problems you don't know how to work.

Third Pass

- If you have time, try to work the most difficult problems.

- Guess at the items you can't work.

- *Do not leave any blanks!*

Usually, time will be running out by the end of your second pass. Don't worry about this. It is *not* critical for you to work every problem on the Math Test. It *is* critical, however, for you to check your work in order to avoid careless mistakes.

Leave NO blanks!

It bears repeating: Do not, under any circumstances, leave an item blank. If you've got a lot left to do when you get the five-minute warning at the end of the test, quickly go back and randomly fill in answers for any blank items. If you find you have time at the end to work more problems, simply erase any incorrect guesses and replace them with the right answers.

Don't try to use special "tricks."

If you know how to do the math, do it. The fastest way through these problems is to do the math, and then find your answer among the choices.

Do not believe any coaching that suggests you can easily find the answers by applying a series of simple tricks. The PSAT/SAT editors go to great lengths to make sure that they catch any items where tricks make a difference. As a result of their careful editing, the application of tricks is usually more difficult than the straight math.

The coaching schools that encourage the use of tricks have developed their own tests to "prove" that the tricks work. They make sure that their practice tests include problems where you can apply their tricks—even if these problems are completely different from the real SAT. If you have coaching materials that do suggest tricks, make sure you try them on an official SAT practice test before you bother to commit them to memory. Take each trick and look through the test for places where it can be applied. With most of the tricks, you'll be surprised at the low number of opportunities for use.

Math Multiple-Choice Tips

You have lots of experience answering multiple-choice questions, so let's focus on some tips that will be helpful specifically on the PSAT and SAT.

 Don't get ambushed by predictable errors.

Imagine a second-grade math class. Here's a problem we want those seven-year-old kids to tackle.

$8 \times 2 = ?$

A)　6

B)　10

C)　16

D)　82

Of course, the correct answer is C. But pay special attention to the other three choices. They are not random numbers. Each one was chosen for a particular purpose.

$8 \times 2 = ?$

A)　6　(subtraction instead of multiplication)

B)　10　(addition instead of multiplication)

C)　16　(correct answer)

D)　82　(putting digits together in complete confusion)

It's easy to see how this works on a simple problem. But standardized test writers do the same thing on more sophisticated problems. In any problem, there are always ways to go wrong. You can choose the wrong operation or regroup incorrectly. You can use the wrong formula or convert a measurement incorrectly. And when you do, the answers you get when making those mistakes will show up as answer choices.

Using these predictable error possibilities is the "dark side" of the Beyoncé or Homer Simpson choices that make questions easier. Predictable error choices make questions harder. That's why it's important to work carefully and check your work thoroughly. If you go wrong in some way, you'll find an answer choice that looks good to you, but it won't be the right one.

It's not always possible to provide three wrong answer choices that are plausible, however. In that case, test-writers have to put in Beyoncé or Homer Simpson choices that are way off. If you are working a problem and you see a choice that seems crazy, *ZAP* it. And before you give up on a super-hard problem, check to see if there are any predictable error choices you can easily *ZAP*. If so, you've raised the odds that your guess will be right.

tip
2

Use the reference information.

At the beginning of the Math Test, you'll see a box labeled "reference information." It contains several formulas that might be used on the test. You should already have them memorized, but it's okay to refer to them during the test if you need to. Not every formula you might need is included: There's nothing about the slope of a line or the area of a trapezoid, for example. Those formulas and others you'll very likely need can be found in the Math Concepts Review section of this book, on pages 74–87.

Here's what the reference information looks like:

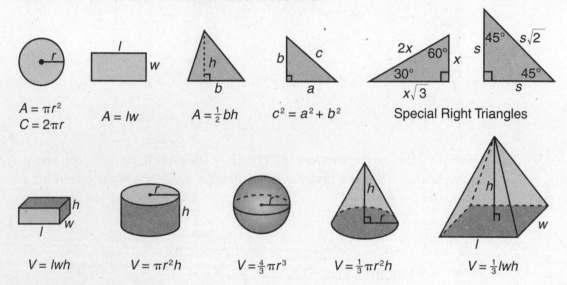

The number of degrees in a circle is 360.
The number of radians in a circle is 2π.
The sum of the measures in degrees of the angles of a triangle is 180.

Try your hand while engaging your mind.

Directions: Use the reference information box to answer the following questions:

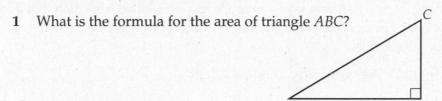

1   What is the formula for the area of triangle *ABC*?

2   Complete this sentence for the above triangle:

$$AC^2 = \boxed{} + BC^2$$

3   What is the sum of the measures of the angles of a triangle?

4   What is the formula for the area of a circle?

5   What is the formula for the circumference of a circle?

6   How many degrees are in the arc of a circle?

7   What is the formula for the area of a rectangle?

8   What is the formula for the volume of a box?

9   What is the formula for the volume of a cylinder?

10   Describe two special right triangles.

Answers are at the bottom of this page.

Treat extended-thinking items as a set, but you don't have to do the items in order.

The test will have at least one extended-thinking item, in which one set of information will be followed by two or more problems. When you get to it, treat each problem separately. You don't need to get the correct answer on one problem to answer the next problem. This is important because a problem set could have a very difficult problem first, followed by a couple of easier problems. If that's the case, you can skip the difficult problem and go straight to the easier ones, then come back to the difficult one at the end.

Caution: If you skip any part of the extended-thinking item at first, try to work it (or guess it) before you move on from the information set. Don't plan to do the rest of the test and then come back. If you do, you'll probably have to reread the information in the set. That's not a terrible thing, but it does take time. It's better to be efficient wherever you can.

1) $c^2 = a^2 + b^2$; 2) AB^2; 3) 180°; 4) πr^2; 5) $2\pi r$; 6) 360°; 7) $l \times w$; 8) $l \times w \times h$; 9) $\pi r^2 h$; 10) 30°-60°-90°, 45°-45°-90°

Write or draw freely in your book.

You will not be allowed to use scratch paper when you take the test, so don't use scratch paper when you take a practice test or use the Workouts that accompany this Study Guide. Get in the habit of writing all over the test booklet. There are three purposes for this:

1) To make sketches and do computations

2) To track your answer sheet—or backtrack if you mess up somewhere

3) To help you concentrate on each item

Check your work on every problem.

It's far more important to avoid careless mistakes than it is to finish all the items. Most students check their work only if they don't find their answer among the choices. This is a bad habit. As we've said before, the errors made on these items are often predictable. It's highly probable that you will find your wrong answer represented among the choices. Don't assume that your answer is correct just because you see it listed. Always, always check your work.

Never create long or complex equations.

There is a straightforward method for solving every problem. If you find yourself in the middle of a long, drawn-out series of computations, you probably set up the problem incorrectly. Go back and rethink your approach to the problem.

Keep moving on the test.

If you get too deeply involved in one problem, you will run out of time and not be able to attain your highest score. With practice, you will learn to recognize the problems that cause long delays for you. Simply skip them and come back later, if you have the time. Make sure you work all the problems that you understand before spending time on the more difficult ones.

Assume all figures are drawn to scale but pay attention!

Unless otherwise stated, all SAT figures are drawn to scale. A side with length 8 will be drawn exactly twice as long as a side with length 4. Once in a while, a drawing will be labeled, "Figure not drawn to scale." When you see that, you may be in luck. The most likely reason the editors didn't draw the figure to scale is because a scale drawing would give the answer away. Try to quickly sketch a more accurate drawing; it might just tell you the answer.

Know how to compute averages.

Almost every test will have at least one or two problems involving averages. To solve these problems, you need to identify three variables: the <u>T</u>otal, <u>A</u>verage, and <u>N</u>umber. (Just think of getting a TAN.)

Usually, the SAT will give you two of these pieces and you must use that information to determine the third piece. Sometimes, you will need to add a list of numbers or do a bit of minor computation to get the first two pieces before you can go after the third piece. Depending on which piece is missing, you'll need to use one of the following simple formulas:

The Total is the Average times the Number $T = A \cdot N$	The Average is the total divided by the Number $A = T/N$	The Number is the Total divided by the Average $N = T/A$

Triple true/false questions can save you time.

These items can take forever if you don't have a strategy for them. However, if you are prepared in advance, they unravel quite easily. Here is an example of the format for this type of item:

> The number 13,023 is evenly divisible by which of the following?
>
>   I.   3
>
>   II. 6
>
>   III. 13
>
> A) I only
>
> B) II only
>
> C) I and II
>
> D) I, II, and III

Much of the time, you won't have to be sure of all three statements. You can often get the right answer just by figuring out two of the three.

Here's how it works. Read the first statement and decide if it's true or false. Before reading the second statement, check the choices to see if you can *ZAP* anything. Repeat this step for the second statement, or, if it's too hard, try the third. You will probably find that you will be able to *ZAP* straight to the correct answer by knowing only two of the three statements.

How to Handle Story Problems

The SAT editors often put simple math in the context of story problems. The method you use to attack story problems must remain flexible because the "best" approach depends on the specific nature of each problem. Keep a clear head; do not let yourself get muddled up. If a problem looks like it's from another planet, skip it, and try the next one. In general, with some variation for each problem, your strategy for story problems should be as follows:

Step 1: Underline the "question" part of the problem first. (Hint: The question is always placed at the end of the story problem.) This will give you a mental framework or context for the problem.

Step 2: Read the whole problem from the beginning, and try to determine what action or operation is taking place. Sometimes the wording is more complicated than seems reasonable, but this is because of the need for precision in the test item. The complicated wording is less of a problem if you follow the advice in Step 1.

Step 3: Pull the math from the problem. Make a sketch or write notes or write a number sentence—anything to get you into the situation and to get the math out of the situation.

Step 4: Reread the problem to make sure your math works.

Step 5: Do the math. Make sure you don't get into complex equations or computation. If you find yourself in the middle of a long, drawn-out process, you're probably working the problem incorrectly. Remember, the SAT and the PSAT do not rely on computation to increase difficulty.

Step 6: Check your answer by plugging it into the original problem. Even if you can't track the math, or if you're running out of time, you must at least check your answer to make sure it's logical in the context of the problem and that you answered the question being asked.

As you practice story problems, ask yourself what kinds of mistakes you are making, then tackle the root of the problem. If you're making a lot of careless mistakes, is it because you forget the original question? Do you make careless calculation errors? It isn't enough to simply say, "I've got to be more careful." If you pay attention to the ways in which you are careless, you will begin to correct these problems.

If you've followed an average track of math courses throughout high school, you've had most of the math on the SAT. Some of your errors are most likely on math that you haven't seen in so long that you forgot you ever knew it or math you didn't understand very well when you first learned it. But don't sell yourself short on the PSAT or SAT math. You probably know more math than you think.

Most people make mistakes on story problems. The mental process goes something like this: *I guess I should know how to do this, but I don't know where to start. Is this algebra or what? How do I even begin to set this problem up?* Many students have difficulty translating the story problems, or "math sentences," into number sentences or equations. Once someone shows you how to set up the equation, you do okay; the problem is that you don't know how to set it up in the first place. If this rings a bell, practice reading story problems and writing them in terms of numbers and variables. Think of this process as "pulling the math" out of the story problem.

Practice Pulling Math out of the Problem (Translating)

The exercises that follow are taken from real SAT problems; some are easy, some are hard. Read the verbal sentences and translate them into number sentences or equations. (We did the first item for you.) Try to understand the relationships between the numbers. If the problem states that one number is five more than the first and ten less than the third, you can express these numbers like this: x, $x + 5$, and $x + 15$.

Try your hand while engaging your mind.

(Answers will vary. Suggested answers are at the bottom of page 67):

1 A. the average of p, q, and r: $\dfrac{p + q + r}{3}$

    B. the average of p and q: $\dfrac{p + q}{2}$

2 A. 3 people working at the same rate for 5 days: _____

    B. 1 of these people working at the same rate for 1 day: _____

3 a team won 54 more games than it lost for a total of 154: _____

4 A. Alan is twice as old as Sue: _____

    B. Alan is half as old as Joseph: _____

    C. the average of Alan, Sue, and Joseph's ages: _____

5 A. Amy is twice as old as Bill: _____

    B. 5 years ago she was 3 times as old as Bill was then: _____

6 A. $\frac{1}{3}$ of a number: _____

    B. $\frac{2}{3}$ of the above number: _____

7 A. the ratio of x to y is 3 to 4: _____

    B. the ratio of y to z is 2 to 1: _____

8 A. the product of 3, 4, and 5: _____

    B. twice the sum of ten and an unknown number: _____

9 A. the length of a rectangle is 3 times its width: _____

    B. the perimeter of this rectangle if its width is x: _____

10 A. the product of two consecutive even integers: _____

    B. product of the same two integers, squared: _____

Once you have determined the number sentence(s) for a problem, ask yourself what you can do with them. If there is an unknown variable, which there probably will be, you will need to set up an equation. Look at the number sentences for your problems. Can you set them up to be equal to each other? Could you set them up to be equal to each other if you added or subtracted a constant from each side of the equation? Does the problem give you the sum or the product of the variables?

Try your hand while engaging your mind.

Directions: Use the 6-step attack strategy to solve the following problems:

1 Amy is twice as old as Bill. Five years ago she was 3 times as old as Bill was then.

How old is Bill now?

2 If three persons who work at the same rate can do a job together in five days, what fractional part of that job can one of those persons do in one day?

If you are having trouble "pulling" or "seeing" the math in these problems, all you need is a little practice. At first, don't concentrate on getting the right answer; instead do your best to set up the number sentences correctly. Get a math teacher or a friend to help you. Once you have mastered this technique, you will be able to concentrate on solving the problems themselves.

1A) given; 1B) given; 2A) $3r \times 5$; 2B) $1r$; 3) $L + (L + 54) = S$; 4B) $A \times 2 = 1$; 4C) $\frac{A + s + 1}{3}$;
5A) $\frac{A}{2} = B$; 5B) $A - 5 = 3(B - 5)$; 6A) $\frac{N}{3}$; 6B) $\frac{N}{3} \times \frac{2}{3}$; 7A) $\frac{X}{Y} = \frac{3}{4}$; 7B) $\frac{Z}{Y} = \frac{1}{2}$; 8A) $3 \times 4 \times 5$; 8B) $2(10+x)$;
9A) $L = 3W$; 9B) $3x + x + 3x + x$; 10A) $a \times (a + 2)$; 10B) $(a \times (a + 2))^2$

Calculator Tips

A calculator is only a tool to save you time. It does not give you knowledge you don't already possess. You still have to think through the problems, whether you're in the calculator section or the non-calculator section of the test.

Here are some tips that will help you on the calculator section of the test.

Bring a familiar calculator to the test.

There's a whole section of the math test that is dedicated to problems using a calculator. The night before the test isn't the time to get a new calculator or to decide to borrow one. Every calculator has its own peculiarities, and you want to be completely comfortable using yours for the test. Be sure to bring your own calculator—don't plan on sharing one with a friend; it's not allowed.

Certain calculating devices are not permitted:

- Cell phone calculators
- Calculators that make noise
- Calculators that need to be plugged in
- Handheld, tablet, or laptop computers

You'll need more than a simple, four-function calculator for the SAT. Check out what's allowed and what isn't by going to the College Board's website: https://sat.collegeboard.org/register/calculator-policy. Practice (starting now) using the calculator you will take with you to the test.

Put in fresh batteries the night before the test—and check to be sure they work. If your calculator dies during the test, don't panic. Just keep working.

Think before reaching for your calculator.

Calculators may increase your speed on some problems, but figuring out how to work the problem is up to you. Don't let your calculator take over what your brain should be doing. Instead of automatically reaching for your calculator, first think through what you need to do to solve the problem. What steps will you need to take? Is there a shorter way to solve the problem?

Avoid careless calculator mistakes.

Calculators can be the source of a lot of careless mistakes, especially if you aren't used to using the one you take to the test. Pay attention to the order of operations (see page 74) and know whether the calculator you are using has the order of operations built in. Probably the next most common mistake is to plug in numbers in the same order they are given in the problem without thinking it through. Other mistakes include not properly clearing your calculator before starting a new problem or punching the wrong number or operation sign. We'll say it again: Pay attention when you use a calculator.

Math Gridded-Response Tips

Practice filling in the grids.

The most important task after figuring out the correct answer is filling in the grid *correctly*. Don't laugh—it's more complicated than you might think. Read the directions carefully (several times) and know them well before you go to the test.

It is always to your advantage to write your answer at the top of the grid before filling in the ovals just as a safeguard against gridding mistakes. What you write in the top of the grid-in box will not be scored, but it will make a difference in your accuracy.

Do not grid-in mixed numbers.

The grid will accept fractions but *not* mixed numbers. An answer of $4\frac{1}{4}$ should be gridded as 17/4 or 4.25. If it is gridded as 4 1/4, the computer will read it as forty-one fourths.

There's no place for negatives or variables.

The grid is not designed to enter a negative answer or an answer with a variable in it. This means all of the grid-in items will be positive values—no negatives or variable expressions. If your answer is a negative number or contains a variable, go back and rethink how you worked the problem. You've definitely done something wrong.

Don't bother reducing fractions.

A time saver! You don't have to reduce fractions to lowest terms; you just have to fit them into the grid (which can contain only four characters, including slashes).

So, if your answer is $\frac{2}{8}$, you do not have to reduce it to $\frac{1}{4}$. Either answer will be accepted.

Be extra careful with repeating decimals.

If your answer turns out to be a repeating decimal or a decimal with more than three digits, include as much of the value in the grid as possible. You must give the most accurate answer that the grid will allow. In other words, use up all the spaces. For example, if your answer is .3333333. . . , grid your answer as .333, not as .33. If your answer is .514285, grid your answer as .514, not .51.

Begin gridding in the far left column.

Actually, if your answer doesn't use all four columns, the SAT scorers couldn't care less where you start gridding. Whether you start on the left or in the middle doesn't matter, as long as it all gets in. But, if you make it a habit to begin gridding your answer in the far left column, you won't make the mistake of leaving off a digit in a repeating decimal.

Some items will have more than one possible answer.

The question usually will indicate this. If you have found an answer that works, use it. You don't have to worry about all the other possibilities.

Practice!

The best way to avoid errors on the grid-in items is to know your math and to practice gridding-in a variety of answers. This will prepare you for test day and help you get through the gridded section more quickly. Use the practice sections to make sure your gridding skills are accurate.

The Most Important Rules

The three most important rules for doing well on the Math Test are:

1) Know your math.

2) Reread every problem.

3) Check your arithmetic.

Sounds too simple, doesn't it? Many of the PSAT and SAT math items can be solved by thinking clearly and logically. However, unless you read carefully, you won't have any chance to "see" the problem. Since the math items require logical reasoning, carelessness at any point may lead you to the wrong answer.

To be sure you're solving the problem you're asked to solve, read every item at least twice. Read every item at least twice. (Notice how this repetition attracted your attention?) The second reading will take only a few seconds, but it may save you several minutes of frustration. As we've said before, SAT items never require lengthy solutions. If you find yourself in the middle of a long procedure, reread the problem.

The third rule is as important as the second. Most students are absolutely annoyed when they find out how many points they've lost due to addition and subtraction mistakes. It often takes only a few seconds to check your arithmetic—and the reward can be a lot of points.

Try your hand while engaging your mind.

Directions: Work the problems below and grid in the answers according to the directions in your Math Workout. Remember, start filling in the grid at the left for best results.

1 What fraction is halfway between $\frac{1}{4}$ and $\frac{1}{5}$?

2 According to the graph, what percent of the people had green eyes?

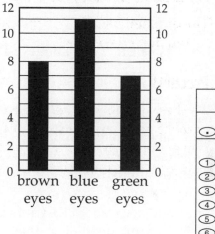

3 What is the perimeter of quadrilateral *ABCD*?

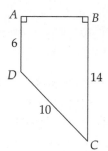

<u>Note</u>: Figure not drawn to scale.

4 If $5x - 8 = \frac{6}{5}$, then what is $5x - 3$?

(1) 9/40; (2) 26.9; (3) 36; (4) 31/5 or 6.2

Error Analysis

One of the things you will learn from practicing for the test is what kinds of errors you make. So after you have done some practice problems, look at the explanations for those problems and see if you can determine why you went wrong. Once you know the kinds of errors you make most often, you can take steps to cut down the number of them, or eliminate them entirely.

Errors come in three flavors:

Error Type E1: "I can't believe I did that!"

This kind of error is the most common for students at all levels of math ability—and it happens most frequently on the easiest questions! E1 errors come from carelessness, sloppiness, or mistakes in basic facts and simple computation. They also come from unfamiliarity with the kinds of problems on the test. And sometimes, E1 errors come from simple anxiety about the test, when students "freeze up" or find themselves unable to think clearly.

The good news about E1 errors is that they don't demonstrate some horrible defect in your math knowledge. They're just test-taking mistakes, and those are easy to fix. You do that by practicing, getting familiar with everything the test can throw at you. (Not only does this build your math knowledge, it also helps eliminate the nervousness.) You do it by checking your work carefully every time, and by doing your best to avoid the predictable errors that always show up as answer choices.

Error Type E2: "I can't remember how to do that!"

This type of error happens when you've seen the same kind of problem before, but you can't remember what to do with it. This is a perfectly normal thing. If you aren't taking an algebra class right now, it's easy to develop some rust on your algebra skills because you're out of practice with it.

These errors are fixable too. If you haven't had algebra for a while, ask a teacher—or your little brother or sister—if you can borrow the textbook you used in the course; do some of the chapter reviews to sharpen your skills. Or, simply look at your old homework (assuming you actually held onto those cherished papers). You'll be surprised how fast it all comes back to you.

The test will contain some problems that require skills you learned long before high school, like working with fractions and exponents. Make sure you're up to date on those skills, too. That's another good reason to refer to the Math Concepts Review on pages 74–87 of this book.

Error Type E3: "I don't think I ever learned that!"

The PSAT and new SAT are intended to focus on the types of math students are doing in school right now as well as the math they will see in the first year of college. But not every student covers the same material at the same time. It's possible that when you take the PSAT or SAT, you will run into some math that you haven't learned yet.

Be ready for this possibility, and don't panic. If you run into a problem that looks like it's written in an alien language, simply take a guess and move on. If you can *ZAP* a choice or two before you do, so much the better. But don't waste a lot of time on a problem that's utterly hopeless. Spend your time on problems you have a chance to get right. Guess on the rest.

Don't waste preparation time before the test trying to learn all the math in the world. Focus your preparation on eliminating E1 and E2 errors, and you'll have more than enough room in your score to absorb a couple of E3 errors.

Your Personal Error-Type Table

After you complete each Math Workout, classify your errors as E1s, E2s, or E3s. Then count the number of each type of error and record it in the table below. Use the table to help focus your practice sessions.

	E1	E2	E3
Math Workout A			
Math Workout B			
Math Workout C			
Math Workout D			
Math Workout E			
Math Workout F			

As you practice, you should see your E1 and E2 errors decrease. Don't worry if your E3 errors stay about the same; you aren't likely to learn a whole new math course in just a month or two.

Chapter 6

Mathematics Content and Concepts Review

Arithmetic and Numeration Concepts

Definitions

Whole Numbers 0, 1, 2, 3, …
Integers … −3, −2, −1, 0, 1, 2, 3, …
Digits 0, 1, 2, 3, 4, 5, 6, 7, 8, 9

Divisibility

A number is divisible by:

2 if it ends in 0, 2, 4, 6, or 8.

3 if the sum of its digits is divisible by 3.

4 if the number formed by the last two digits is divisible by 4.

5 if it ends in 0 or 5.

6 if it is divisible by both 2 and 3.

7 (sorry, no easy rule)

8 if the number formed by the last three digits is divisible by 8.

9 if the sum of its digits is divisible by 9.

The Order of Operations

You can use **PEMDAS** to help you remember the order of operations. (Or, you can simply remember this sentence: "**P**lease **E**xcuse **M**y **D**ear **A**unt **S**ally.")

1. **P**arentheses. Work everything inside parentheses first. Within the parentheses, follow the other rules.

2. **E**xponents. Simplify all powers and roots next.

3. **M**ultiplication and **D**ivision. Perform any multiplication and division, from left to right.

4. **A**ddition and **S**ubtraction. Perform any addition and subtraction, from left to right.

74

Even and Odd Numbers

Adding
even + even = even
even + odd = odd
odd + odd = even

Multiplying
even × even = even
even × odd = even
odd × odd = odd

Absolute Value

The absolute value of a number is the number's distance from zero on a number line. Because absolute value is a distance, it is always a positive number. The absolute value of 0 is 0. The symbol for the absolute value of x is $|x|$.

$$|5| = 5 \qquad |-5| = 5 \qquad |0| = 0$$

Fractions

Addition

Fractions must have common denominators before you can add them. Find a common denominator. For each fraction, find the equivalent fraction that has the common denominator. Then add the numerators.

Example:

$$\frac{1}{3} + \frac{2}{5} = \frac{5}{15} + \frac{6}{15} = \frac{11}{15}$$

Subtraction

Fractions must have common denominators before you can subtract them. Find a common denominator. For each fraction, find the equivalent fraction that has the common denominator. Then subtract the numerators.

Example:

$$\frac{3}{4} - \frac{1}{2} = \frac{3}{4} - \frac{2}{4} = \frac{1}{4}$$

Multiplication

Fractions do NOT need common denominators before you can multiply them. Multiply the numerators, then multiply the denominators.

Example:

$$\frac{3}{5} \times \frac{2}{3} = \frac{6}{15}$$

Division

Fractions do NOT need to have common denominators before you can divide them. To divide a fraction by another fraction, multiply the first fraction by the reciprocal of the second fraction. To find the reciprocal of a fraction, switch its numerator and denominator.

Example:

$$\frac{1}{4} \div \frac{1}{3} = \frac{1}{4} \times \frac{3}{1} = \frac{3}{4}$$

Percents

Percent means hundredths, or number out of 100.

Examples:

$$\frac{30}{100} = 30\%$$

2 is 25% of 8 because $\frac{2}{8} = \frac{25}{100} = 25\%$

Converting decimals to percents

Move the decimal point two places to the right and insert a percent sign.

Examples:

0.09 = 9%   0.85 = 85%

0.007 = 0.7%   2.13 = 213%

Converting a fraction $\frac{x}{y}$ to a percent

$$\frac{x}{y} = \frac{z}{100}$$

Example:

$$\frac{2}{5} = \frac{z}{100}$$

$$z = 100\left(\frac{2}{5}\right)$$

$$z = 40\%$$

Finding percent of a number

Change the percent to a decimal and multiply.

Example:

What is 20% of 50?

0.20 x 50 = 10.00 = 10

Ratios

Read "m is to n" and written m:n or $\frac{m}{n}$.

Rate

A **rate** is a ratio that compares two different kinds of numbers, such as dollars per hour or miles per gallon. A unit rate has a 1 as the denominator of the ratio.

Example:

Heidi read 30 pages in 2 hours. She reads at a rate of 15 pages per hour.

$$30 : 2 = \frac{30}{2} = 15$$

Proportions

A **proportion** is two rates that are equal to each other. Read "c is to d as s is to t." This is written as:

$$\frac{c}{d} = \frac{s}{t}$$

You can find the missing term of a proportion by cross-multiplying.

Example:

$$\frac{c}{50} = \frac{75}{250}$$

$$250c = 75 \times 50$$

$$250c = 3,750$$

$$c = 15$$

Exponents

Positive exponents

$$3^4 = 3 \times 3 \times 3 \times 3 = 81$$

Negative exponents

$$2^{-3} = \frac{1}{2^3} = \frac{1}{2} \times \frac{1}{2} \times \frac{1}{2} = \frac{1}{8}$$

NOTE: $x^1 = x$ and $x^0 = 1$ when x is any number other than 0.

Multiplication/Division

To multiply exponents, if the base numbers are the same, keep the base number and add the exponents.

Example:

$$4^3 \times 4^2 = 4^5$$

To divide, if the base numbers are the same, keep the base number and subtract the second exponent from the first.

Example:

$$5^7 \div 5^3 = 5^4$$

When the base numbers are not the same, first simplify each number with an exponent, then multiply or divide.

Examples:

$$4^2 \times 3^3 = 16 \times 27 = 432$$

$$4^2 \div 2^2 = 16 \div 4 = 4$$

Addition/Subtraction

Whether or not the base numbers are the same, you must simplify each number with an exponent before performing the operation.

Examples:

$5^2 + 3^3 = 25 + 27 = 52$

$6^2 - 2^4 = 36 - 16 = 20$

NOTE: If a number with an exponent is raised to another power, keep the base number and multiply the exponents.

Example:

$(6^3)^4 = 6^{12}$

Algebra Concepts

Definitions

polynomial: an expression that has variables with exponents that are positive whole numbers; no term of the polynomial will have a variable in its denominator

linear equation: an equation that can be written as $ax + b = 0$.

linear function slope intercept form: $y = mx + b$, where x and y are variables, m is the slope, and b is the y-intercept (where the line crosses the y-axis)

quadratic equation: an equation that can be written as $ax^2 + bx + c = 0$

function: a special relationship (like an equation) in which each input will have exactly one output

system of equations: a set of equations that are solved at the same time

inequality: a statement which shows that two values are not equal
$>$ means "is greater than" and $<$ means "is less than"

Complex Numbers

A complex number is a number that can be expressed as $a + bi$, where a and b are real numbers and i is the imaginary unit. The imaginary unit is a solution to the equation $x^2 = -1$, and it is usually written as i, such that $i = \sqrt{-1}$.

Examples:

$4 + 2i$ $\qquad\qquad$ $6 - 3i$

Multiplying Polynomials

To multiply two binomials (an algebraic expression with two terms), use the FOIL method. FOIL stands for <u>F</u>irst, <u>O</u>utermost, <u>I</u>nnermost, and <u>L</u>ast.

Step 1. Multiply the <u>F</u>irst terms from each binomial.

Step 2. Multiply the <u>O</u>utermost terms.

Step 3. Multiply the <u>I</u>nnermost terms.

Step 4. Multiply the <u>L</u>ast terms from each binomial.

Step 5. Simplify if necessary.

Example:

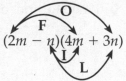

$(2m - n)(4m + 3n)$

Step 1: First

$2m \bullet 4m = \mathbf{8m^2}$

Step 2: Outermost

$2m \bullet 3n = \mathbf{6mn}$

Step 3: Innermost

$-n \bullet 4m = \mathbf{-4mn}$

Step 4: Last

$-n \bullet 3n = \mathbf{-3n^2}$

Step 5: Simplify

$8m^2 + 6mn - 4mn - 3n^2 = \mathbf{8m^2 + 2mn - 3n^2}$

Solving Quadratic Equations

To solve a quadratic equation:

Step 1. Set the quadratic equal to zero.
Step 2. Factor.
Step 3. Set each factor equal to zero.
Step 4. Solve each of these equations.
Step 5. To check your work, insert each answer into the original equation.

Example:

$x^2 + 7x = -10$

1. $x^2 + 7x + 10 = 0$

2. $(x + 2)(x + 5) = 0$

3. $x + 2 = 0$ or $x + 5 = 0$

4. $x = -2$ or $x = -5$

5. $(-2)^2 + 7(-2) =$ $(-5)^2 + 7(-5) =$

$4 + (-14) = -10$ $25 + (-35) = -10$

Using the Quadratic Formula

You can use the quadratic formula to solve quadratic equations. For a quadratic equation $ax^2 + bx + c = 0$, the quadratic formula is:

$$\frac{-b \pm \sqrt{b^2 - 4ac}}{2a}$$

Example:

$y^2 + 7y = -10$

$y^2 + 7y + 10 = 0$

$$\frac{-7 \pm \sqrt{49 - 4(1)(10)}}{2(1)} = x$$

$$\frac{-7 \pm \sqrt{49 - 40}}{2} = x$$

$$\frac{-7 \pm \sqrt{9}}{2} = x$$

$$\frac{-7 \pm 3}{2} = x$$

$x = -\dfrac{10}{2}$ or $x = -\dfrac{4}{2}$

$x = -5$ or $x = -2$

Inequalities

Treat inequalities (such as $7x + 4 > 32$) just like equations, with one exception: When multiplying or dividing both sides by a negative number, you must reverse the direction of the sign.

Solving Systems of Equations in Two Variables

When you solve a system of equations in two variables, you find values for the variables that are true for all the equations in the system. To solve a system of equations, find the value of one variable, then use that to find the value of the other variable.

Step 1. Choose one of the equations to work with.
Step 2. Isolate one variable in that equation.
Step 3. Substitute the value of this variable into the second equation.
Step 4. Solve for the other variable.
Step 5. Use the value of this variable to find the value of the first variable.

This sounds complicated, but it's really not.

Example:

Solve this system of equations:

$y + 6x = 15$

$4x - 3y = 21$

Step 1. Choose one equation: $y + 6x = 15$
Step 2. Isolate one variable: $y = -6x + 15$
Step 3. Substitute: $4x - 3(-6x + 15) = 21$
Step 4. Solve for x: $4x + 18x - 45 = 21$

$22x = 66$

$x = 3$

Step 5. Find the value of y: $y + 6(3) = 15$

$y + 18 = 15$

$y = -3$

The solution for the system of equations is $(3, -3)$.

Solving a Function

When you solve a function, treat $f(x)$ the same way you would treat y. Solve $f(x) = 3x - 5$ the same way you would solve $y = 3x - 5$.

The Coordinate Plane

On the coordinate plane shown below, the horizontal and vertical lines are called the coordinate axes, or the x-axis and the y-axis. The coordinate plane is divided into quadrants, labeled by Roman numerals I, II, III, and IV. The numbers in parentheses (called ordered pairs) represent points on the coordinate plane. The ordered pair $(0, 0)$ represents the origin.

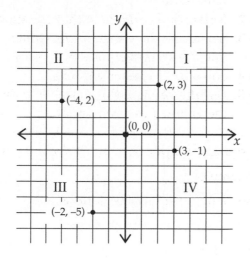

For point $(-4, 2)$, -4 is the x-coordinate and shows how far the point lies to the left or right of the origin; 2 is the y-coordinate and shows how far the point lies above or below the origin.

Slope of a Line

To find the slope of a line in a coordinate plane, use the following formula:

$$\text{slope} = \frac{\text{the difference in the } y\text{-coordinates of any two points on the line}}{\text{the difference in the } x\text{-coordinates of the same two points on the line}}$$

or simply stated:

$$\text{slope} = \frac{\text{rise}}{\text{run}} \text{ or } \frac{y_2 - y_1}{x_2 - x_1} \text{ where } (x_1, y_1) \text{ and}$$
(x_2, y_2) are points on the line.

When the slope is positive, the line goes up from left to right. When the slope is negative, the line goes down from left to right.

Graphing a Linear Equation

The graph of a linear equation is a straight line. It's easy to graph a linear equation if you get it into the form $y = mx + b$.

x and y can be any ordered pair on the line.

m is the slope of the line.

b is the y-intercept (where the line crosses the y-axis).

Example:

Graph the equation $12x + 3y = 6$

First put the equation into the proper form and simplify:

$$12x + 3y = 6$$
$$3y = -12x + 6$$
$$y = -4x + 2$$

The y-intercept is 2, so the line crosses the y-axis at 2. One ordered pair on the line is (0, 2).

The slope is −4. To find another point, go down 4 and right 1. To find a third point, once again go down 4 and right 1.

Draw a line through these three points.

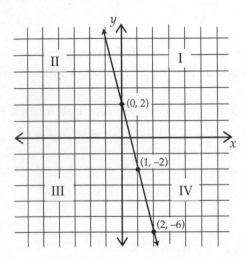

Graphing a Quadratic Equation

The graph of a quadratic equation $(y = ax^2 + bx + c)$ is called a parabola. It looks like the letter U, either right side up or upside down.

x and y can be any ordered pair on the parabola. a, b, and c can have any value, except a cannot equal zero.

Geometry Concepts

Lines and Angles

Parallel lines are lines in the same plane that never intersect. Parallel lines are denoted by the symbol | |.

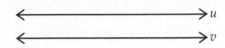

Perpendicular lines intersect to form right angles and are denoted by the symbol ⊥.

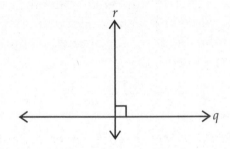

A **right angle** measures 90 degrees.

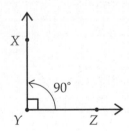

A **straight angle** measures 180 degrees.

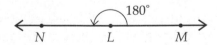

Adjacent angles share a common vertex and a common side.

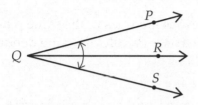

∠*PQR* and ∠*RQS* are adjacent angles.

Complementary angles are two angles whose measures have a sum of 90 degrees.

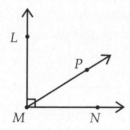

∠*LMP* and ∠*PMN* are complementary angles.

Supplementary angles are two angles whose measures have a sum of 180 degrees.

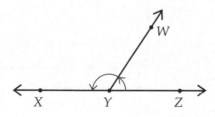

∠*XYW* and ∠*WYZ* are supplementary angles.

When two lines intersect, four angles are formed. The angles opposite each other are called **vertical angles** and their measures are equal. In the example below, the measures of angles 1 and 3 are equal, and the measures of angles 2 and 4 are equal.

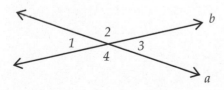

An example of **two parallel lines cut by a third line** (called a *transversal*) is shown below.

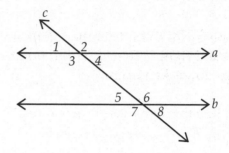

Angles 1 and 5 are called **corresponding angles** and their measures are equal.

Angles 3 and 6 are called **alternate interior angles** and their measures are equal.

Angles 2 and 7 are called **alternate exterior angles** and their measures are equal.

Similar Figures

Similar figures are the same shape but not the same size. The ratios of the lengths of corresponding sides of similar figures are equal. The measures of corresponding angles of similar figures are equal.

Example:

△ *ABC* and △ *EFG* are similar.

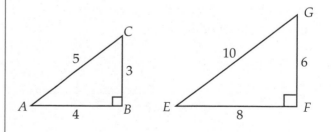

Congruent Figures

Congruent figures are the same shape and the same size. The lengths of corresponding sides of congruent figures are equal. The measures of corresponding angles of congruent figures are equal.

Example:

>   Figure *FGHJ* and Figure *WXYZ* are congruent.

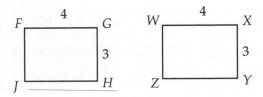

Triangles

The sum of the measures of the angles of a triangle is always 180 degrees.

The sum of the lengths of any two sides of a triangle must be greater than the length of the third side.

A triangle with all three sides the same length is called an **equilateral triangle**. Each angle of an equilateral triangle measures 60 degrees.

$$n + n + n = 180$$
$$3n = 180$$
$$n = 60$$

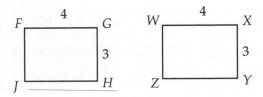

A triangle with two sides of equal length is called an **isosceles triangle**. Two of the angles in an isosceles triangle (those opposite the equal sides) are also of equal measure.

$$\angle a = \angle b$$

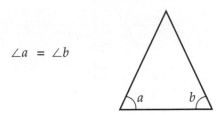

A triangle with one of its angles measuring 90 degrees is called a **right triangle**. The relationship between the lengths of the three sides of a right triangle is described by the **Pythagorean Theorem**.

The Pythagorean Theorem

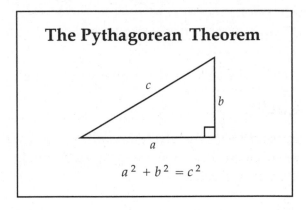

$$a^2 + b^2 = c^2$$

Example:

>   If $a = 6$, $b = 8$, and $c = 10$,
>
> $$a^2 + b^2 = c^2$$
> $$6^2 + 8^2 = 10^2$$
> $$36 + 64 = 100$$
> $$100 = 100$$

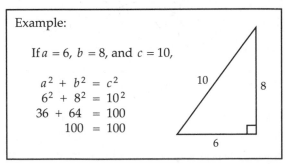

The ratio of the sides of a right triangle with angles 30°, 60°, 90° is 1:$\sqrt{3}$:2.

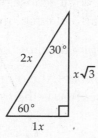

The ratio of the sides of an isosceles right triangle with angles 45°, 45°, 90° is 1:1:$\sqrt{2}$.

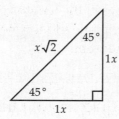

Circles

In the circle below, $\overline{AB}$ is the **radius** and $\overline{AC}$ is the **diameter**. The distance around the circle is the **circumference**.

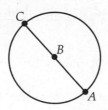

For a circle of radius r:

> **Circumference** $= 2\pi r = \pi d$

The number of degrees of arc in a circle is 360.

Area, Perimeter, and Volume Formulas

Area of a rectangle: = length × width

Area of a triangle: = $\frac{1}{2}$ (base × altitude)

Area of a trapezoid: = $\frac{1}{2}(b_1 + b_2)$ height

For a circle with radius r: Area = πr^2

Perimeter of a rectangle = 2 (length + width)

Volume of a rectangular solid: = length × width × height

Data Analysis Concepts

Measures of Center

Measures of center help you to analyze a set of data. You can use the measures of center to describe a set of data using only one value. There are three measures of center you should know:

Mean (often called the average)

To find the mean, add all the numbers in the data set and divide by the number of numbers.

> Example:
>
> Aruna scores 9, 6, 12, 7, 6 on her quizzes. What is the mean of her quiz scores?

Add the scores, then divide by the number of scores.

$$\frac{9 + 6 + 12 + 7 + 6}{5}$$

$$= \frac{40}{5}$$

$$= 8$$

The mean (average) of Aruna's quiz scores is 8.

Median (think of it as the middle value)

Put the numbers in order from least to greatest. If there is an even number of numbers, add the middle two and divide by 2.

> Example:
>
> Aruna scores 9, 6, 12, 7, 6 on her quizzes. What is the median of her quiz scores?
>
> Put the scores in order from least to greatest.
>
> 6, 6, 7, 9, 12
>
> The middle number is 7. Aruna's median score is 7.

If she took another quiz and scored 8, the middle two numbers would be 7 and 8. Her median score would be $\frac{7 + 8}{2} = 7.5$.

Mode (think of it as the most common)

In a group of numbers, the number that appears the most often is the **mode**.

> Example:
>
> Aruna scores 9, 6, 12, 7, 6 on her quizzes. What is the mode of her quiz scores?
>
> Which score did Aruna receive most often? 6
>
> The mode of Aruna's quiz scores is 6.

A data set can have *no* mode if all the numbers appear the same number of times. It can also have *more than one mode*, if two or more numbers appear the same number of times and the most times in the data set.

Measures of Spread

Measures of spread are another way to describe data using one value. There is one measure of spread you should know for the test:

Range

The range of a set of data is the difference between the largest number in the set and the smallest.

> Example:
>
> Aruna scores 9, 6, 12, 7, 6 on her quizzes. What is the range of her quiz scores?
>
> The largest number is 12. The smallest is 6.
>
> $12 - 6 = 6$
>
> The range of Aruna's quiz scores is 6.

Data Representations

There are different ways to present data. Some work better than others in specific situations. You probably remember line graphs, bar graphs, and circle graphs. Here are a few others you should definitely know:

Scatterplot

A **scatterplot** looks a little bit like a coordinate plane, and it works kind of like one, too. A scatterplot shows the relationship between two sets of data.

This scatterplot shows the relationship between hours studied and SAT score.

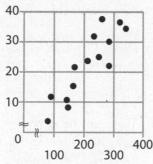

A **line of best fit** helps show a correlation between two related sets of data.

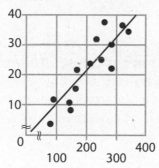

Two-Way Frequency Tables

A two-way table shows the frequencies of relationships between two sets of variables.

Children's Favorite Trees

	Oak	Willow	Redwood	Total
3 years old	17	3	52	72
4 years old	20	16	39	75
5 years old	2	3	77	82
Total	39	22	168	229

Histogram

Use a histogram instead of a bar graph when you want to show the numerical values of continuous variables. A histogram is similar to a bar graph, with important differences.

If you want to show the number of oak trees in a city's parks, use a bar graph.

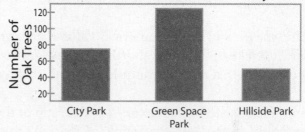

If you want to show the heights of children in a preschool class, use a histogram.

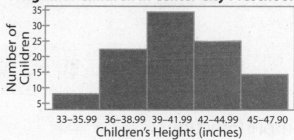

The bars on a bar graph have spaces between them because the data are discrete. The bars on a histogram have no spaces between them because the data are continuous.

The trees are each discrete variables. The children's heights are continuous variables.

Trigonometry Concepts

All of the basic *trigonometric functions* are numbers (often to several decimal places) that express the ratios of two sides in a *right* triangle for one of the two smaller *angles* (10°, 45°, 89°, 16.5°, $x°$, *theta*, etc.) in the right triangle.

The three sides of a triangle for trig purposes are:
1. the side *opposite* the angle in question
2. the side *adjacent* to the angle in question (other than the hypotenuse)
3. the *hypotenuse*, the longest side, the side opposite the 90° angle

The *sine* (or *sin*) is the numerical value that expresses the ratio of the side *opposite* the angle to the *hypotenuse*, or in trig shorthand, *opposite over hypotenuse*. It is important to remember the word *over*. In a typical example, the sine of 45°, or sin 45°, is equal to .7071.

You form a *fraction* that expresses the ratio of the two sides. Often, this is all you need to do. In a right triangle with an angle of 45°, the three sides have the ratio $1:1:\sqrt{2}$. Thus the sine of 45° equals 1 *over* the square root of 2, or .7071.

Most of the work can be done using the Pythagorean Theorem ($a^2 + b^2 = c^2$) once the basic definitions are known. The SAT usually uses special triangles in test items that simplify the work, such as "3, 4, 5 triangles," "5, 12, 13 triangles," "30°, 60°, 90° triangles," etc. A basic rule of trig is: $sin(x)^2 + cos(x)^2 = 1$.

> ### There are only SIX trig functions you need to know!

Simple Functions

First, the three *simple* functions:
1. *sin* (sine) of an angle = opposite over hypotenuse ($s = \frac{o}{h}$, or **soh**)
2. *cos* (cosine) of an angle = adjacent over hypotenuse ($c = \frac{a}{h}$, or **cah**)
3. *tan* (tangent) of an angle = opposite over adjacent ($t = \frac{o}{a}$, or **toa**)

Start by memorizing this mystical expression:

> ### SOH, CAH, TOA

Chant this phrase fifty or a hundred times until it is burned into your brain.

Reciprocal Functions

Finally, the last three functions, the *reciprocal functions*:

These functions (*cotangent, secant, cosecant*) are reciprocals of the first three. A **reciprocal** is a fraction with its numerator and denominator reversed.

The reciprocal of $\frac{3}{4}$ is $\frac{4}{3}$.

The three reciprocal functions can also be derived by dividing various sides of right triangles by each other, but there is a simpler way to derive them. Each is just the reciprocal of one of the three simple functions:

4. *cot* (cotangent) of an angle $= \dfrac{1}{\tan}$

5. *sec* (secant) of an angle $= \dfrac{1}{\cos}$

6. *csc* (cosecant) of an angle $= \dfrac{1}{\sin}$

It follows that if one of the simple functions equals $\frac{3}{5}$ or .6000, its reciprocal equals $\frac{5}{3}$.

The **reciprocal ratio** is the result, therefore, of the side that is 5 *over* the side that is 3.

Once you know the basics, you can work your way back to anything else you need to find (sides, angles, other functions, etc.) by using the Pythagorean Theorem and your knowledge of right triangles and fractions and by labeling the various sides and angles of the triangle in a drawing. Sometimes you can get the answer just by inverting a fraction, and you won't need to draw the right triangle.

All you need to remember is the information in the box below, being careful not to confuse the different functions. It would be a good idea to write them in your exam book at the first opportunity.

> SOH, CAH, TOA
>
> $\cot = \dfrac{1}{\tan}$, $\sec = \dfrac{1}{\cos}$, $\csc = \dfrac{1}{\sin}$

Radians

Radians are angle measures based on arc length in a circle with radius of 1. A 360° angle (a full circle) has 2π (pi) radians because the arc length (circumference) is $2\pi r$. So any fraction of that 360° central angle, measured in radians, will be that same fraction multiplied by 2π.

For example: $60° = \dfrac{60}{360} \cdot 2\pi r = \dfrac{2\pi}{6}$ radians. Remember:

> **360° $= 2\pi$ radians**

Chapter 7

The Evidence-Based Reading Test

The official name of the PSAT/SAT Reading Test is Evidence-Based Reading, but that's simply what *every* standardized reading test is. You'll be asked questions about what you read, and you'll have to use evidence you find in the passage to answer those questions.

What to Expect

On the SAT Reading Test, you'll be required to make inferences and draw conclusions based on evidence from the text. You may be asked to—

Test	Passages	Questions	Minutes
PSAT	5	47	60
SAT	5	52	65

- Evaluate main ideas and identify critical details
- Compare and contrast ideas and link causes and effects
- Describe how text structure contributes to meaning
- Identify the author's purpose and how the author tries to influence the reader's thinking
- Define words in context and discuss how word choice affects meaning

What Types of Passages Will Be on the Test?

- One or two science passages
- One or two history or social studies passages
- One literature passage
- One of the above passages might be a set of paired passages, which are two short passages that are related in some way.
- One of the history/social studies passages could be an excerpt from an American "Founding Document."

Reading Strategy Tips

 tip 1   **Take control of the combined SAT Reading and Writing and Language sections.**

We'll say this again, because it's so helpful to keep in mind: The first step in taking control of the SAT Reading and Writing and Language sections is to shorten both subtests to fit your personal situation. It makes no difference if you score your points on the Reading section or the Writing and Language section. The sections are combined to get your SAT score, and a point on one section counts the same as a point on the other.

If your starting score is around 400, don't fantasize about moving up to a 600. Instead, think in terms of moving up gradually. The number of problems you need to work and double-check depends on your target score. The following table shows what you need to do to hit various target levels.

Reasonable Target SAT Reading & Writing Score	To take control of the Reading & Writing and Language Test, you need to be . . .
790–800	correct on 50 Reading questions and 44 Writing questions. You need to *ZAP* and then guess on the 2 remaining questions.
710–730	correct on 40 Reading questions and 40 Writing questions. You need to *ZAP* and then guess on the 16 remaining questions.
610–630	correct on 30 Reading questions and 30 Writing questions. You need to *ZAP* and then guess on the 36 remaining questions.
510–530	correct on 20 Reading questions and 20 Writing questions. You need to *ZAP* and then guess on the 56 remaining questions.
430–450	correct on 10 Reading questions and 10 Writing questions. You need to *ZAP* and then guess on the 76 remaining questions.
380–400	correct on 5 Reading questions and 5 Writing questions. You need to *ZAP* and then guess on the 86 remaining questions.

For example, if your reasonable target is an SAT Reading & Writing Section score of 520, you need to use as much time as necessary to work and double check 20 of the 52 Reading questions and 20 of the 44 Writing questions—even if it takes nearly all of your test time. In the remaining minutes of each section, *ZAP* and then guess on the other 56 questions. (32 Reading and 24 Writing). On average, you'll pick the right answer about 14 times out of 56 blind guesses. Using the SAT Conversion Tables, you estimated SAT Score will be about 520.

The key to making this system work is to be perfect on the number of problems that you work and double-check. Careless mistakes can ruin your SAT Score.

You don't have to do the passages in order.

As we just said, some passages will be harder to read and more time-consuming, so take a little time to rearrange the passages on the Reading Test into an order that benefits you. As you work through the Reading Test, if you come to a Founding Document, or some other passage that seems especially difficult, skip it. Come back to it after you've worked through all of the other passages. Just be sure you also skip those item numbers on your answer sheet. You don't want to get off track or you'll lose points.

If you put the hardest reading passage last, you'll gain two benefits:

1) By doing the easier passages first, you'll get those points safely in the bank.

2) If you find yourself running out of time on the Reading Test and have to guess on the last passage, you'll be guessing on the passage you were least likely to do well on anyway.

You might not want to do all five passages.

Believe it or not, a few students might benefit from *not even trying to answer the questions* on the hardest passage and simply marking random guesses for the questions on it. Seriously.

Here's why.

If you guess on 10 questions (which is the approximate number you will find with each reading passage), you can expect to get two or three guesses right simply because of the law of averages. On a Founding Document, most students will be lucky to get two or three questions right even if they're trying, so it isn't as though you'll be throwing 10 points away if you guess on them.

Plus, not wasting time plowing through difficult prose will give you more time to spend on the remaining passages. This increases the likelihood that you'll get more of those questions right. Chances are good that you'll gain more points in the long run by doing it this way.

In this, however, as in all things, the final decision is up to you. If you tend to read more slowly when taking a test, you'll probably be better off doing your best on four of the five passages and blind guessing or *ZAPPING* on the fifth. On the other hand, if you're a fast reader who understands what you read on the first try, you definitely should try to read all the passages and answer all the questions. After all, that's the only way to get a perfect score.

Be prepared for challenging text.

Most of the passages on the redesigned SAT Reading Test will feel like current magazine articles or textbook chapters. But a few of them will probably contain some old-fashioned language. For example, your literature passage may have been written by Jane Austen or another 19th-century novelist. These passages are sometimes a little challenging to understand, but generally not impossible for most readers.

The College Board has made a lot of noise about how they're going to provide at least one passage from America's "Founding Documents." These could be taken from the Constitution, the Declaration of Independence, the *Federalist Papers*, or possibly from a document such as Thomas Paine's *Common Sense* or George Washington's Farewell Address.

Or, your test might include a document the College Board designates as contributing to what they call the Great Global Conversation. These include works by writers such as "Edmund Burke, Henry David Thoreau, Gandhi, Elizabeth Cady Stanton, and Martin Luther King Jr."

If you happen to get one of the Founding Documents on your test, you may well find it difficult to understand without concentrated effort. The prose style used by educated people in the late 1700s, when these documents were written, was much different from what we're used to reading now. It will help if you have read some of the Founding Documents in your history classes, but even then, the reading will probably be pretty challenging.

The College Board goes on to say, "Although the founding documents and Great Global Conversation texts are historical in nature, it is important to note that all of the information needed to answer the associated Reading Test questions is found in the passages themselves." Further, the College Board may include a note explaining the historical context of the time in which it was written.

Keep your pencil active as you read.

Let's be real. You're likely to find the passages fairly dull. They're supposed to be representative of college-level material, which means you can expect them to be fairly dense and complicated— a sure-cure for insomnia.

It's in your best interest to make sure the passages don't lull you to sleep. One way to keep your brain engaged (and awake) is to keep your pencil active while you read. By staying actively engaged with what you're reading, you will probably be able to understand it better, which makes answering the questions easier.

Believe it or not, every student won't find the reading passages boring. For example, let's imagine you're a dedicated fan of all things biology. In your test, you come across a passage that describes the history of the treatment of mitochondrial cytopathies (crazy unlikely, but you never know). Hooray! You're overjoyed at finding a topic you can sink your teeth into.

If that happens, consider yourself one lucky student. Just don't get so excited that you start to daydream about your scientific career and that Nobel Prize you're going to win someday. Just read the passage. Answer the questions. And quickly move on.

There is no firm rule about how to mark up your text. Here are some ideas to consider.

- **Underline** the main idea or topic sentence of the passage and/or paragraphs.
- **Circle** things that seem to be important, like the first mention of names, places, and significant dates.
- **Make notes** in the margin to clarify confusing or long-winded concepts.
- **Draw lines** to connect actions or thoughts to the person they belong to.
- **Number** the sequence of events in order, but watch for out-of-sequence actions such as "but first…" and "before that…." Words that define sequence, like *first*, *second*, *earlier*, and *later* link events together.
- **Mark** expressions that define opinions, like *he feels* and *she thinks*.

Don't worry about marking "just the right things." You aren't being graded on it. The goal of underlining, circling, and so on is to help you focus on the passage and follow the logic. Marking up the passage can also help you spend less time looking at the passage trying to find answers.

Use keywords to connect ideas in the passage.

Pay close attention to keywords in the passage. Keywords link ideas together and identify relationships between different ideas in the passage. (We call them *keywords* even though some of them are phrases.) If you're taking the test on paper, circle the keywords in the passage. If you're taking the test on a computer, highlight the keywords.

Reversal Words	Supporting Words	Result Words
on the other hand	additionally	because
however	since	so
yet	moreover	consequently
rather	besides	therefore
in spite of	furthermore	thus
nevertheless	in fact	accordingly
despite		as a result
instead		resulting
notwithstanding		
but		
although		

- **Reversal words** link ideas that are opposite or contradictory. "Taking a bite out of a super-hot pepper seemed like a good idea, *but* now Ryan is sorry he did it."

- **Supporting words** link ideas that support one another (how about that?) or that follow one after the other. "Ryan is sorry he ate that pepper; *in fact*, he says he may never eat anything spicy again."

- **Result words** signal cause and effect. "Ryan ate the entire quart of ice cream while trying to put the fire out in his mouth, *therefore* we aren't having any dessert tonight."

Make a mental map of the passage as you read.

Read the passage carefully, but don't belabor it. The passage will not be snatched away from you when you get to the questions, so don't try to memorize it. Read carefully but quickly, making a mental map of the passage as you go. When you get to the questions, you will need a good grasp of the main idea of the passage and where to go in the passage to find a few details.

Many of the questions will contain specific line references, but these don't always tell you where to find the correct answer. Line references often remind you where a quote comes from or where an idea was first introduced. But you may not find the answer to that particular question for several lines or even paragraphs. You will still need to know the general layout of the passage to get to the correct answers.

Read the whole passage before looking at the questions.

Have you heard that it's best to read the questions before you read the passage? That would be a great idea on some tests, but not on the SAT. Reading the questions first means that you have to read the questions twice, which takes way too much time.

Resist the temptation to read only part of the passage and then jump into the questions. SAT reading questions require you to think and reason about what you have read. Careless readers are easily caught by wrong choices on the reading questions.

Do not try to memorize the whole passage. And don't stop reading near the end. Read thoroughly but quickly, *then* go to the questions. Many students are so anxious to get started on the questions that they quit reading about halfway through the passage. Bad idea!

Answer every question about the passage before moving on.

Don't skip around in the Reading Test. And don't save a reading question thinking you'll come back to it later. If you don't know the answer to a question after you've just read the passage, will you know it after reading another passage and answering several more questions? Probably not. Answer all of the questions for a passage while the passage is still fresh in your mind. Then you can move on to the next passage with a clear head.

Don't expect the correct answer to restate the passage word for word.

The SAT is designed to test your reading comprehension skills, not whether you can find a specific detail in a passage. Sometimes answers are stated directly, but more often they will be hinted at. This happens in various ways—through a collection of details, by the author's tone, by a character's or subject's own words, and so on.

The right answer to a question will never come out of the blue. There must always be something in the passage (evidence!) you can point to that makes you think an answer is correct. The paired questions, which we'll discuss on page 96, are an example of this—but you will do it with every question on the Reading Test, at least to a certain extent. In other words, you don't always have to *show* what makes you think an answer is right, but there always has to be something there.

Read the following paragraph from *Western Political Heritage* by William Y. Elliott and Neil A. McDonald, and the question that follows it:

> Sparta, which had grown from an organization of conquerors, was by its location less exposed to the influence of trade. . . . Sparta developed into a civilization more like that of modern Junker Prussia, that is, feudal landlords bound together by holding down their serfs, or helots. The organization of Sparta
> 5 always reflected internal tension by the necessity of remaining perpetually armed, as much against internal revolution from the helots, who were the conquered older inhabitants, as against external attack.

The authors imply that the helots were

A) privileged.

B) cruel.

C) confused.

D) rebellious.

The answer to an inference question will always be consistent with the main idea of a passage. Any choice that goes beyond the facts of the passage, or seems like it jumps to a conclusion, isn't going to be the right answer.

The authors never come right out and say that the helots were rebellious, but they provide some useful facts. The landowning Spartans were "bound together by holding down" the helots (Lines 3 and 4). The Spartans remained "perpetually armed" (Lines 4–6) to guard against "internal revolution" (Line 6). And the authors say that the helots were the "conquered older inhabitants" of the area (Lines 6 and 7). Taken together, that's a lot of evidence that the Spartans faced a potential rebellion. Choice D is correct.

Many questions will ask you to interpret information that is implied in the passage, rather than specifically stated. The SAT editors want to see if you understand what you read, not whether you can regurgitate information word for word.

On paired passages, do the first passage first.

The Reading Test will contain five passages and question sets, but sometimes one of the longer science or social studies passages will be replaced with two shorter passages that are related in some way. There will be questions about each individual passage and about the two passages together.

Attack the paired passages in this order:
Step 1. Read Passage 1.
Step 2. Answer the questions related only to Passage 1.
Step 3. Go back up and read Passage 2.
Step 4. Answer the questions related only to Passage 2.
Step 5. Finally, answer the questions that ask you about both passages.

Why do it this way? Because the questions are always in this order. Questions about Passage 1 come first. Questions about Passage 2 come next. And questions about both passages together come last. Always. So why not use that to your advantage?

If you read both passages before answering the questions, you'll have to keep all that information in your memory. Answering the questions about the first passage first frees up space in your brain to concentrate on the second passage. You're less likely to get the two passages confused. After working on each passage separately, you can go back and consider both passages together.

Think of passage comparison questions as a double true/false.

Some questions may ask you to compare a pair of passages. For example, a question may ask if a statement is true for both passages. Think of this as a double true/false question. If it's not true for Passage 1, *ZAP* any choices that say it is. If it's not true for Passage 2, *ZAP* those choices. Then go back to the passages to find information that will help you choose the right answer from the remaining choices.

Use True/False clues for ZAPPING. Watch for giveaway words in some of the choices.

If you are having trouble solving the problem as a multiple-choice test item, think of it as four true/false questions. Look at each choice as a true or false statement. Three statements are false—only one statement is true.

Check for words that would give away one or two of the choices as false statements.

Examples of Absolute Words (usually indicate false statements)	**Examples of Ambiguous Words** (more likely to appear in true statements)
all	some
always	often
every	may
must	seem
no	most
never	usually
none	many

The following item presents an opportunity to *ZAP* on the basis of giveaway words. This strategy should be applied only in situations where you don't have time to read the passage or where you have already read the passage but it didn't make any sense to you.

Which of the following most accurately states the artist's position as implied by the first sentence of the passage?

A) Every piece of art is equally worthy of praise.

B) Art is an activity that supersedes most others.

C) All innovative art is attractive to the general public.

D) Art and society usually influence each other.

 tip

14

Answer paired questions as a set.

Expect to see some paired questions on the Reading Test. The first one will look like a regular comprehension question. The fun starts when you get to the second question in the pair. Here's an example.

 16

The author suggests that one major effect of carbon nanotube semiconductors will be
A) stronger steel.
B) new diseases.
C) faster travel.
D) thinner hardware.

 17

Which choice provides the best evidence for the answer to the previous question?
A) Lines 5–9 ("In the six . . . great promise.")
B) Lines 5–18 ("One important . . . a tube.")
C) Lines 30–33 ("Imagine . . . of paper.")
D) Lines 30–33 ("Space scientists . . . earth orbit.")

Reading passages are numbered every five lines, and the words in parentheses are the opening and closing words of parts of the passage that you need to pay attention to. The choices refer you to four places in the text that might offer evidence for the answer you've chosen for the previous question.

Paired questions will be easier to do if you treat them as a set. Here's a list of steps to follow when you're confronted with them:

1) Look at the passage to find out where the first question is discussed, and answer the question based on what you find there.

2) Draw a line under the words in the text that answer the question.

3) Write the item number or make a mark in the margin to help you locate the underlined section when you go back to the question and answer choices.

4) Look at the choices for the second question in the pair. If there's a line reference that matches—or nearly matches—where you found the answer to the first question, that's almost certainly the answer for the second question.

If you're able to answer the first question of the pair correctly, the three wrong answers for the second question will seem like Homer Simpson choices. That's the good news. The bad news is, if you miss the first one, you're pretty likely to miss the second one, too. So, if you are unsure that your answer to the first question is correct, verify by looking for each line reference in the second question.

Graphs, charts, and tables aren't just on the math test anymore.

Reading test passages will occasionally be accompanied by a graph, a chart, or a table with quantitative information related to the passage. You could be asked to interpret information straight out of the graphic, or to explain how information in the graphic relates to something that appears in the passage.

You've had plenty of experience with graphs, charts, and tables in your math and science classes, and the data sets that appear on the Reading Test will seem familiar. Here's a quick refresher on how to attack them:

• Read the title and any introductory text.

• On a bar or line graph, determine what's shown on the horizontal and vertical axes, and what the minimum and maximum values are.

• On a pie chart, determine how the pieces are labeled and look at their relative sizes.

• On a table, read the titles of each column and determine whether you can find a pattern in the data.

Often, questions about data sets will ask you whether a statement in the passage is supported by the data. Don't assume that the passage is correct; the data may contradict the passage. Trust your ability to read the graphics and answer the question accordingly.

For multiple meaning words, identify the part of speech before deciding on the correct meaning.

Unlike previous years, when juniors had to memorize words and definitions they wouldn't encounter except in college or graduate school, today you'll need to understand how to use vocabulary words that you see every day. But don't be fooled; you can still make mistakes if you're not on guard. The Reading Test will ask about familiar words that have a number of different meanings, and you will be required to choose the proper meaning for the context.

Imagine a passage that contains the following sentence in Line 15:

> Shauna wasn't able to raise the issue of a salary increase because her boss was out of town.

As used in Line 15, *raise* most nearly means

A) compensation.

B) improvement.

C) lift.

D) discuss.

The answer choices present four different meanings of *raise*. If you're having trouble deciding which one is right, think about this first: What part of speech is the target word? In this sentence, *raise* is a verb. (It can be used as a noun, but that's not the case here.)

Do you see any other verbs in the answer choices? Two of our choices — *lift* and *discuss* — are verbs, but the other two, *compensation* and *improvement*, are nouns. You might expect that Shauna would want to talk with her boss about her *compensation* or an *improvement* in her salary, but those are predictable errors. *Compensation* and *improvement* are nouns, but we're looking for a verb. *ZAP* A and B. What about C, *lift*? *Lift* is a verb that can also be a noun, as in *Give me a lift*. Because it can be a verb, we'll consider that form in this context. But *lift* doesn't make sense in this context. *ZAP* C. Does it make sense that Shauna might try to *discuss* an issue with her employer? Sure, it does.

An even more accurate choice than *discuss* might have been the word *mention*, as *to raise an issue* is the same as *to mention an issue*, but *mention* is not an answer choice that's available to us.

Following are examples of multiple-meaning words like those you might see on the test. Be sure you understand the differences in meaning, especially when the words appear as different parts of speech. It's not a comprehensive list of every multiple-meaning word you might see on the test. It's only a sample. You can (and should) find (and study) more extensive lists. Look for them online or in your school library.

bear	coast	demand	grave	low
capture	common	direct	great	plastic
challenge	conduct	document	hold	reason
chance	convey	embrace	interest	store
channel	crop	favor	issue	turn
charge	deep	form	lounge	view

Multiple-Meaning Words Activity

Directions: Write sentences for each word in the pairs below, using the correct meaning and specified part of speech. (You can change the form of a word as needed by adding a suffix such as *-ed* or *-ing*.)

1   table (noun)

_____

_____

  table (verb)

_____

_____

2   slight (adjective)

_____

_____

  slight (verb)

_____

_____

3   direct (verb)

_____

_____

direct (adjective)

_____

_____

4   pitch (verb)

_____

_____

pitch (noun)

_____

_____

5   drive (noun)

_____

_____

drive (verb)

_____

_____

drive (noun)

_____

_____

When time is running out, look for questions that provide line or paragraph references.

These questions can usually be answered without reading any more than a small portion of the passage.

Appendix

Ultimate Challenge

Guessing—Case Study #1

The SAT Math Test includes a total of 58 items. What if you knew 38 answers and blindly guessed on the other 20 items? On average, students will gain five raw score points from blind guessing on 20 items. Add 5 points to your raw score to show what you would likely earn by guessing on the remaining items.

Case Study #1 TOTAL SAT MATH TEST SCORE		
	RAW SCORE	SAT SCORE
Without Guessing	38	
With Blind Guessing		

Your instructor will help you estimate your SAT score in this example. Fill that number in the boxes when prompted.

Seminar Activity

The Ultimate Challenge on the facing page is based on the 20 hardest Math questions ever to appear on the SAT. These questions represent situations where many students need to guess.

In this activity, we've eliminated several of the wrong answers. Your job is to choose the correct answers from the choices remaining. Wait until your instructor tells you to begin. Then circle the correct answer choices as quickly as you can.

It Can't Hurt!

When you aren't sure of the answer, guess.

No matter how poorly you guess, any difference will always be in the positive direction. You can't hurt your score by guessing.

When you're guessing, do so quickly. A fast guess is just as good as a slow guess.

The Ultimate Challenge				
1	A	B	C	D
2	A	B	C	D
3	A	B	C	D
4	A	B	C	D
5	A	B	C	D
6	A	B	C	D
7	A	B	C	D
8	A	B	C	D
9	A	B	C	D
10	A	B	C	D
11	A	B	C	D
12	A	B	C	D
13	A	B	C	D
14	A	B	C	D
15	A	B	C	D
16	A	B	C	D
17	A	B	C	D
18	A	B	C	D
19	A	B	C	D
20	A	B	C	D

Write the number you got correct in the box below.

Raw Score on The Ultimate Challenge with Elimination

12/20

The Effects of Eliminating Choices on the SAT

If we gave this Ultimate Challenge to a million students, the average score would be 11. If your score was higher or lower than 11, it was simply by chance.

The Ultimate Challenge clearly demonstrates that not all guessing is alike. The only difference between blind guessing and the Ultimate Challenge is that some of the choices were eliminated on the Ultimate Challenge. This helped you zero in on the right answer.

On the real SAT and PSAT, you can often eliminate one, two, or three choices—even when you don't know the correct answer. Use what you do know to *ZAP* the answer choices that are definitely wrong. Cross them out in your test booklet (putting a slash mark through the choice letter is enough) so you don't have to consider them again, then pick from the ones that remain.

Guessing—Case Study #2

Just like Case Study #1, let's say you knew 38 answers on the SAT Math Test. You again had to guess on the other 20 items. This time, instead of blind guessing, you were able to eliminate some of the choices first.

In other words, you zeroed-in on the answers and then picked from the leftovers. You were guessing on both tests—but on the Ultimate Challenge you were guessing between fewer choices. The average gain on the Ultimate Challenge is 11 extra points from zeroing-in before guessing. Go ahead and add 11 to the initial raw score of 38. Enter that number in the correct box in the table below. Your instructor will tell you what your new SAT score would be.

Case Study #2 The Effects on Guessing on the SAT Test		
	RAW SCORE	**SAT SCORE**
Without Guessing	38	600
With Blind Guessing	43	640
With Eliminating Choices		

If you eliminate choices before you guess, you increase your odds of getting the correct answer—*and* your score will go up! We call this way of eliminating choices *ZAPPING*. (See page 6 for more information.)

Scoring

Estimating Your SAT Scores

Enter your Workout Scores in the table below. Your seminar instructor will explain how to use your scores and the tables on pages 105–107 to calculate your estimated SAT scores.

Writing Number Correct	
Workout A	15/21
Workout B	18/22

Reading Number Correct	
Workout A	17/19

Math Number Correct	
Workout A No Calculator	4/10
Workout A Calculator Permitted	8/20

Mathematics Score Conversion

The *ZAPS* Math Workouts provide an easy estimation of your SAT mathematics score:

Step 1: In Table 1 (page 105), find your Number Correct (1–10) on Workout Section A (without calculators) and your Number Correct (1–20) on Workout Section B (calculators allowed).

Step 2: Convert the Number Correct to the estimated SAT Math Score Scale, circling the intersecting cell of the Number Correct on Workouts A and B.

For example:

> Pat answered 7 questions correctly on Workout A and 14 questions correctly on Workout B. Using Table 1, move down Column 7 to Row 14. Pat's estimated SAT Math score range is 600–620.

Evidence-Based Reading and Writing Score Conversion

When combined, the *ZAPS* Reading Workouts and Writing and Language Workouts provide an estimate of the SAT Evidence-Based Reading and Writing Section score:

Step 1: In Table 2 (page 106), find your Number Correct on One Reading Workout.

Step 2: Draw a loop around the Number Correct and your Estimated Reading Score Range in Table 2.

Step 3: In Table 3 (page 106), find your Number Correct on One Writing Workout.

Step 4: Draw a loop around the Number Correct and the Estimated Writing and Language Score Range in Table 3.

Step 5: Use **Table 4** (pages 106–107) to convert the score ranges to an Estimated SAT Writing & Language Score. First, circle the range for your Reading Score. Next, circle the range for your Writing Score. The estimated SAT range is the lowest to the highest score within the intersecting cells.

For example:

> Jan answered 14 questions correctly on the Reading Workout and 19 questions correctly on the Writing Workout. Using Table 2, Jan's *Estimated Reading Score* is 31–32. Table 3 shows Jan's *Estimated Writing Score* to be 34–34 (it's still called a *score range* even when the "range" is simply one number). Using Table 4, Jan draws a loop around her Estimated Reading score in columns 31 and 32. Then she draws a loop around her estimated Writing and Language score in row 34. The intersection of columns 31 and 32 with row 34 shows a high estimate of 660 and a low estimate of 650. Jan's estimated SAT Evidence-Based Reading and Writing Score range is 650–660.

TABLE 1

Estimated Math Score Range (Using Number Correct
on two math sections: with and without calculators)

Number Correct on Math Workout A (no calculators)

Number Correct on Math Workout B (calculators allowed)

	10	9	8	7	6	5	4	3	2	1
20	780–800	760–780	740–760	710–740	690–700	670–680	660–670	630–650	570–600	570–600
19	760–790	740–760	710–740	690–710	670–690	660–670	640–660	620–640	600–620	570–600
18	740–760	710–740	690–710	670–690	660–670	640–660	620–640	600–620	590–600	570–590
17	710–740	690–710	670–690	660–670	640–660	620–640	600–620	590–600	570–590	560–570
16	690–710	670–690	660–670	640–660	620–640	600–620	590–600	570–590	560–570	540–560
15	670–690	660–670	640–660	620–640	600–620	590–600	570–590	560–570	540–560	520–540
14	660–670	640–660	620–640	600–620	590–600	570–590	560–570	540–560	520–540	510–520
13	640–660	620–640	600–620	590–600	570–590	560–570	540–560	520–540	510–520	490–510
12	620–640	600–620	590–600	570–590	560–570	540–560	520–540	510–520	490–510	480–490
11	600–620	590–600	570–590	560–570	540–560	520–540	510–520	490–510	480–490	470–480
10	590–600	570–590	560–570	540–560	520–540	510–520	490–510	480–490	470–480	450–470
9	570–590	560–570	550–560	530–550	520–530	500–510	480–490	470–480	450–470	430–450
8	560–570	550–560	530–550	520–530	500–520	480–500	470–480	450–470	430–450	410–430
7	550–560	530–550	520–530	500–520	480–500	470–480	450–470	430–450	410–430	380–410
6	530–550	520–530	500–520	480–500	470–480	450–470	430–450	410–430	380–410	360–380
5	520–530	500–520	480–500	470–480	450–470	430–450	410–430	380–410	360–380	330–360
4	500–520	480–500	470–480	450–470	430–450	410–430	380–410	360–380	330–360	310–330
3	480–500	470–480	450–470	430–450	410–430	380–410	360–380	330–360	310–330	280–310
2	470–480	450–470	430–450	410–430	380–410	360–380	330–360	310–330	280–310	240–280
1	450–470	430–450	410–430	380–410	360–380	330–360	310–330	280–310	240–280	210–240

[Handwritten notes:]
reading 590–690
math 600–730
470–480
real
510–520

TABLE 2
Estimated Reading Score Range

Number Correct on One Reading Workout

19	40–40
18	38–39
17	37–37
16	35–36
15	33–34
14	31–32
13	30–31
12	29–30
11	27–28
10	25–26
9	24–25
8	23–24
7	21–22
6	20–21
5	19–19
4	17–18
3	15–16
2	12–14
1	10–11

TABLE 3
Estimated Writing & Language Score Range

Number Correct on One Writing Workout

22	39–40
21	38–38
20	35–37
19	34–34
18	32–33
17	31–32
16	30–30
15	28–29
14	27–28
13	26–26
12	25–25
11	23–24
10	22–23
9	21–21
8	19–20
7	18–19
6	16–17
5	15–16
4	13–14
3	12–13
2	10–11
1	10–10

690 – 700

TABLE 4
Estimated Evidence-Based Reading and Writing Score Range

Score Range for Reading Test (See Table 2)

Score Range for Writing Test (See Table 3)

	40	39	38	37	36	35	34	33	32	31	30	29
40	800	790	780	770	760	750	740	730	720	710	700	690
39	790	780	770	760	750	740	730	720	710	700	690	680
38	780	770	760	750	740	730	720	710	700	690	680	670
37	770	760	750	740	730	720	710	700	690	680	670	660
36	760	750	740	730	720	710	700	690	680	670	660	650
35	750	740	730	720	710	700	690	680	670	660	650	640
34	740	730	720	710	700	690	680	670	660	650	640	630
33	730	720	710	700	690	680	670	660	650	640	630	620
32	720	710	700	690	680	670	660	650	640	630	620	610
31	710	700	690	680	670	660	650	640	630	620	610	600
30	700	690	680	670	660	650	640	630	620	610	600	590
29	690	680	670	660	650	640	630	620	610	600	590	580
28	680	670	660	650	640	630	620	610	600	590	580	570
27	670	660	650	640	630	620	610	600	590	580	570	560
26	660	650	640	630	620	610	600	590	580	570	560	550
25	650	640	630	620	610	600	590	580	570	560	550	540
24	640	630	620	610	600	590	580	570	560	550	540	530
23	630	620	610	600	590	580	570	560	550	540	530	520
22	620	610	600	590	580	570	560	550	540	530	520	510
21	610	600	590	580	570	560	550	540	530	520	510	500
20	600	590	580	570	560	550	540	530	520	510	500	490
19	590	580	570	560	550	540	530	520	510	500	490	480
18	580	570	560	550	540	530	520	510	500	490	480	470
17	570	560	550	540	530	520	510	500	490	480	470	460
16	560	550	540	530	520	510	500	490	480	470	460	450
15	550	540	530	520	510	500	490	480	470	460	450	440
14	540	530	520	510	500	490	480	470	460	450	440	430
13	530	520	510	500	490	480	470	460	450	440	430	420
12	520	510	500	490	480	470	460	450	440	430	420	410
11	510	500	490	480	470	460	450	440	430	420	410	400
10	500	490	480	470	460	450	440	430	420	410	400	390

TABLE 4 continued
Estimated Evidence-Based Reading and Writing Scale Score Range

Score Range for Reading Test (See Table 2)

Score Range for Writing Test (See Table 3)

	28	27	26	25	24	23	22	21	20	19	18	17	16	15	14	13	12	11	10
40	680	670	660	650	640	630	620	610	600	590	580	570	560	550	540	530	520	510	500
39	670	660	650	640	630	620	610	600	590	580	570	560	550	540	530	520	510	500	490
38	660	650	640	630	620	610	600	590	580	570	560	550	540	530	520	510	500	490	480
37	650	640	630	620	610	600	590	580	570	560	550	540	530	520	510	500	490	480	470
36	640	630	620	610	600	590	580	570	560	550	540	530	520	510	500	490	480	470	460
35	630	620	610	600	590	580	570	560	550	540	530	520	510	500	490	480	470	460	450
34	620	610	600	590	580	570	560	550	540	530	520	510	500	490	480	470	460	450	440
33	610	600	590	580	570	560	550	540	530	520	510	500	490	480	470	460	450	440	430
32	600	590	580	570	560	550	540	530	520	510	500	490	480	470	460	450	440	430	420
31	590	580	570	560	550	540	530	520	510	500	490	480	470	460	450	440	430	420	410
30	580	570	560	550	540	530	520	510	500	490	480	470	460	450	440	430	420	410	400
29	570	560	550	540	530	520	510	500	490	480	470	460	450	440	430	420	410	400	390
28	560	550	540	530	520	510	500	490	480	470	460	450	440	430	420	410	400	390	380
27	550	540	530	520	510	500	490	480	470	460	450	440	430	420	410	400	390	380	370
26	540	530	520	510	500	490	480	470	460	450	440	430	420	410	400	390	380	370	360
25	530	520	510	500	490	480	470	460	450	440	430	420	410	400	390	380	370	360	350
24	520	510	500	490	480	470	460	450	440	430	420	410	400	390	380	370	360	350	340
23	510	500	490	480	470	460	450	440	430	420	410	400	390	380	370	360	350	340	330
22	500	490	480	470	460	450	440	430	420	410	400	390	380	370	360	350	340	330	320
21	490	480	470	460	450	440	430	420	410	400	390	380	370	360	350	340	330	320	310
20	480	470	460	450	440	430	420	410	400	390	380	370	360	350	340	330	320	310	300
19	470	460	450	440	430	420	410	400	390	380	370	360	350	340	330	320	310	300	290
18	460	450	440	430	420	410	400	390	380	370	360	350	340	330	320	310	300	290	280
17	450	440	430	420	410	400	390	380	370	360	350	340	330	320	310	300	290	280	270
16	440	430	420	410	400	390	380	370	360	350	340	330	320	310	300	290	280	270	260
15	430	420	410	400	390	380	370	360	350	340	330	320	310	300	290	280	270	260	250
14	420	410	400	390	380	370	360	350	340	330	320	310	300	290	280	270	260	250	240
13	410	400	390	380	370	360	350	340	330	320	310	300	290	280	270	260	250	240	230
12	400	390	380	370	360	350	340	330	320	310	300	290	280	270	260	250	240	230	220
11	390	380	370	360	350	340	330	320	310	300	290	280	270	260	250	240	230	220	210
10	380	370	360	350	340	330	320	310	300	290	280	270	260	250	240	230	220	210	200

Answer Explanations

Writing Workout A

1 B Using a preposition to join these clauses is awkward (choices A, C, D). It's clearer to make the clauses two separate sentences.

2 C Amanda Petrusich's extensive experience writing about music makes her a credible authority about rare blues recordings.

3 A The sentence as it appears is more precise and colorful than any of the other choices. In addition, choice B is too casual for a formal essay.

4 D When referring to people, use *who* instead of *that* (choice A) or *which* (choice B). The word *whom* is incorrect because the people described here are not the objects of an action.

5 C Even if you have never heard of these musicians, it's reasonable to expect you to recognize *Skip James*, *Blind Blake*, and *Robert Johnson* as full names, especially since *Skip James* was mentioned in the first sentence. Names in series should be separated by commas.

6 B The pronoun *its* refers to the blues artists, so the plural pronoun *their* is correct. Expect to be checked on the use of *its* versus *it's*, though neither is correct here.

7 D Because sentence 4 begins with *They*, leaving it where it is now (A) or placing it before sentence 1 (B) makes it unclear what *They* is referring to. Placing the sentence after sentence 1 (C) causes a discussion of *obscure artists* to be interrupted by a discussion of rare *records*, only to be followed by a list of specific artists (*Skip James*, *Blind Blake*, and *Robert Johnson*). Placing the sentence after sentence 2 gives *They* its proper referent (*collectors*), and offers support for the idea that record collectors are most interested in extremely rare recordings.

8 B The two sentences present contrasting ideas, but choices A and D signal a cause-and-effect relationship. Starting the sentence with *Unfortunately* (C), prepares the reader to expect something disappointing, which isn't sustained by the rest of the paragraph. Only choice B correctly sets up the contrast.

You may note that all the choices except B are followed by a comma. A comma is optional after *yet* when used in this way. Don't worry, you won't be asked to choose between a comma and no comma when either is correct.

9 A The sentence amplifies the point the author is making in the paragraph, so it should be added here. Choice B is incorrect because it contradicts the author's point that collectors often equate the rarity of a recording with its value. Choice C is incorrect because it's true that the sentence contradicts the idea that non-rare recordings are unimportant, but that is a reason for including the sentence, not leaving it out. The sentence is on-topic for the paragraph, so choice D is incorrect.

10 D The fact that people wanted to buy original Delta blues numbers is implied in the previous sentence. It's not necessary to repeat it. And, the fact that there *was a market for* Delta blues means they *were highly salable*, making choice B even more redundant.

11 A *Stature* means *status* or *standing*; thanks to modern collectors, acoustic blues has high standing today, but that doesn't necessarily reflect the way the people of the 1930s viewed acoustic blues. *Statute* is a law. *Statue* is a sculpture. And *state* can be either a nation or territory or a condition at a given time. Be very careful when presented with words that look or sound alike.

12 B *Mankind* is a collective noun, and collective nouns can be singular or plural depending on context. In this case, each of us is part of humanity, so it's proper to use the plural pronoun *we*.

13 C Choices B and D are false. Choice A would be true if it weren't for the fact that the chart shows no maneuvers recorded in 2013. Even though there were no maneuvers recorded in 2013, it's correct to say that the trend is "mostly upward" since 2010.

14 A The most precise topic sentence for the paragraph is the one that already appears (choice A). There's no evidence in the passage to support choice B. Making the ISS safer (choice C) is only one of the benefits of the proposed system. Choice D is a detail that's stated later in the paragraph; this is an example of the need to pay attention to the context surrounding an underlined sentence.

15 A Choice B is not appropriate for a formal essay. Choice C is redundant. Choice D implies that something is wrong with the ISS and needs to be *fixed*, which is neither implied nor stated in the passage.

16 C Sometimes it takes only a small fix to effectively revise a larger piece of text. It makes the most sense to say that the telescope will find and target pieces of debris (choice C). Debris must be found before it can be targeted by the laser. Choices A and B get this relationship backward. Choices B and D are awkward.

17 D Choices A and C create run-on sentences. Choice B is awkward because the word *there* is better placed with the next independent clause.

18 D The ideas expressed in the first two sentences contrast with one another. The team is not proposing entirely new hardware; *instead* of entirely new hardware, the system will use some existing hardware.

19 B *Deployed* (choice B) is all that's needed. Anything deployed aboard the ISS would have to be launched into space, so choices A and C are redundant. It's not strictly necessary to define *deployed* (choice D), but if the author wanted to do so, "put on the ISS" isn't a strong-enough definition.

20 C Choice A incorrectly combines a past-tense word, *was*, with the future tense *to be*. Choice B uses the past tense to talk about something that is in the future. Choice D sets up the expectation that something happening in the second half of the sentence will have an effect on what's happening in the first half of the sentence; in fact, the opposite is true. It might be possible to build a laser-equipped spacecraft in the future, but only if the ISS-based system is successful first.

21 D   The sentence discusses the full-sized system's proposed effectiveness. This sentence best supports the information in sentence 4 and leads into the information found in sentence 5. Both sentences 4 and 5 refer to the size of the laser and telescope, as does the sentence the writer is planning to add.

22 B   Choice B helps the reader understand why the *Daily Mail* called the system "the REAL Death Star." Choices A and C are off-topic with the rest of the passage. Choice D would be a better fit elsewhere in the passage.

Writing Workout A Item Breakout

ITEM	KEY	SKILL	CONTENT DIMENSION
1	B	Sentence formation	Sentence structure
2	C	Precision	Effective language usage
3	A	Precision	Effective language usage
4	D	Conventional expression	Usage
5	C	Items in series	Punctuation
6	B	Possessive determiners	Usage
7	D	Logical sequence	Organization
8	B	Introductions/conclusions/transitions	Organization
9	A	Support	Development
10	D	Concision	Effective language usage
11	A	Frequently confused words	Usage
12	B	Agreement	Usage
13	C	Quantitative information	Development
14	A	Proposition	Development
15	A	Style and tone	Effective language usage
16	C	Logical sequence	Organization
17	D	End-of-sentence punctuation	Punctuation
18	D	Introduction/conclusion/transition	Organization
19	B	Concision	Effective language usage
20	C	Shift in construction	Sentence structure
21	D	Logical sequence	Organization
22	B	Introduction/conclusion/transition	Organization

Writing Workout B

1 **C** The compound subject of this clause is *one expert or another*, which is singular. One expert *suggests*, or another expert *suggests*. For *suggest* to be correct (A), the subject would have to be plural: *experts suggest*. That's also true of choice B, which uses the plural verb *have*. Choice D is awkward as well as implausible; you're not likely to find something that hasn't yet been suggested.

2 **B** Items in series should be separated with commas. Semicolons (choice D) are not appropriate unless the series items are extremely long or contain commas themselves. In addition, this sentence requires you to understand that *American studies*, *English literature*, and *archaeology* are separate subjects, which is not clear in either choice A or choice C.

3 **B** Choice A is redundant and choice D is too wordy. The second-person pronoun *yourself* in choice C is inappropriate when attached to a statement in the third person.

4 **D** Choices A, B, and C are not appropriate transitional words in this spot because they are supporting words that would strengthen the argument in the previous paragraph. The second paragraph is actually a reversal of the first paragraph, in which any transition word would need to reflect the change in direction. Since no reversal word is among the choices, the best option is to simply start the paragraph with the question.

5 **C** *Marshal* as a noun (A) refers to a law enforcement officer; as a verb it means "to arrange or assemble." In American English, *Marshall* (B) is generally seen only as a surname. The adjective *martial* (C) refers to combat; a martial artist, like Bruce Lee, is someone who practices karate, judo, and/or similar forms of physical combat. *Marital* (D) is an adjective referring to marriage.

6 **B** The phrase as *Clinton, Allen, King, or Lee might* is a nonrestrictive phrase, which could be removed from the sentence without affecting the meaning. Such phrases can be set off by commas or dashes, but such punctuation should never be mixed (a problem choice C creates). A colon (D) can be used to introduce a statement, but it's not the proper option in context here.

7 **C** This sentence doesn't fit at this point; it would go better at the end of the first paragraph (C). Choices A and B are incorrect because the sentence is off-topic for the paragraph and doesn't provide a good transition. In fact, the sentence interrupts the transition that begins the next paragraph. The sentence doesn't work as a conclusion for the entire passage (D)—it actually contradicts the main point of the passage.

8 **C** Choice A is too informal for an essay of this type, but Choice B is awkwardly phrased. The most straightforward option, C, is best. Choice D is also short, but it's not the proper word in that spot. In English, we don't say that someone *understands* a skill; however, we do say that someone *learns* a skill (choice C).

9 **A** This sentence requires careful reading. The counselor is using her education as a philosopher as a sounding board for two things: her clients' reflections and her own reflections. It would be clearer if she said it that way, but "my clients' and my own reflections" is correct as constructed.

10 A According to the chart, a philosophy graduate earns more than both an architecture and a marketing graduate by mid-career, so choice B is false. Choice C is false because the chart shows a government graduate's early career salary is about $45,000 compared to just over $40,000 for a philosophy graduate. Choice D may be true, but there's no information in the chart to support it.

11 D The paragraph sets up a contrast. It starts by talking about practical and sought-after careers such as architecture and marketing, then observes that some philosophy graduates drive buses or work in retail stores, which are less-well-paid careers. Then comes the contrasting part: some people with the most practical and desirable college degrees also drive buses or work in retail stores. The conjunction *but* is the only option that makes the contrast between the two ideas clear. This isn't an either-or situation (B) nor a cause-and-effect relationship (C).

12 B No punctuation is needed between *game* and *after*. Choice A makes no sense. Choices C and D create fragments.

13 A Kennedy enrolled at Harvard, which is one university, correctly referred to with the singular possessive pronoun *its*. B is a plural pronoun. If you chose C, you probably confused *it* with *their*. The word *it's* is a contraction, not a pronoun; you can expect to be tested on the use of *it's* and *its* or similar homophones.

14 C The sentence as it appears (choice A) and choice D are sentence fragments. Choice B doesn't clarify the writer's intent but instead muddles it with clunky construction. Choice C eliminates the comma and the pronoun *who*, which clarifies the intent of the sentence.

15 B *So* (choice A) and *so that* (choice C) imply that Nixon's lack of success at football was due to his education. Choice D implies a contrast between clauses of the sentences, but there is no contrast. Choice B creates the proper relationship to suggest that while Nixon played college football, he wasn't very good at it.

16 D *Had maintained* (A) implies that it happened in the past and was over, but it's clear from the passage that Nixon loved football throughout his life. Nixon *maintained* a love of football throughout his life. It was an ongoing action. *Throughout his life* implies that Nixon is no longer living, so that eliminates choices B and C.

17 A Parallel structure requires both verbs in the underlined part of the sentence to be treated the same way. Choice A is the simplest construction and provides us with parallel construction in the verbs *played* and *coached*.

18 C Choice C is the clearest way to state that while Nixon was running for president in 1968, he considered asking Lombardi to be his vice president, but only for a short time. Choice A is missing the subject of the sentence, *he* or *Nixon*. Choice B has the modifier, *briefly*, in the wrong place, implying that his question to Lombardi was *brief*. Choice D is awkward construction.

19 B The sentence as underlined is awkwardly constructed. Choice C flips the clauses but is still awkward. Choice D doesn't make much sense. Choice B puts the information about the importance of football to Nixon and his frequent application of its terminology to politics in the right places.

20 D *Mess* (choices A and B) is too casual to use in a formal essay. The word *hijinks* (C) means *boisterous fun*, hardly a fitting description for a crime serious enough to lead to the president's resignation.

21 A The preceding sentence discusses Nixon's enjoyment of football talk. Choices B and C have nothing to do with this. Choice D is off-topic for the paragraph. Choice A offers an example of how football served as a conversation topic for Nixon.

22 D The paragraph begins by saying that Ford was a far more successful football player than Nixon and details his accomplishments. Choice D makes the point that while playing pro football would have represented the pinnacle of achievement in that field, the presidency represents the pinnacle of achievement for a politician. Choice B is simply an interesting fact. Choice C mentions that Nixon and Ford *would cross paths again*, but there is no mention in the passage of their having crossed paths a first time, so it makes no sense.

Writing Workout B Item Breakout

ITEM	KEY	SKILL	CONTENT DIMENSION
1	C	Agreement	Usage
2	B	Items in series	Punctuation
3	B	Concision	Effective language usage
4	D	Introduction/ conclusion/ transition	Organization
5	C	Frequently confused words	Usage
6	B	Nonrestrictive and parenthetical elements	Punctuation
7	C	Focus	Development
8	C	Style and tone	Effective language usage
9	A	Possessive nouns and pronouns	Punctuation
10	A	Quantitative information	Development
11	D	Sentence formation	Sentence structure
12	B	Unnecessary punctuation	Punctuation
13	A	Possessive determiners	Usage
14	C	Sentence formation	Sentence structure
15	B	Sentence formation	Sentence structure
16	D	Shift in construction	Sentence structure
17	A	Sentence formation	Sentence structure
18	C	Sentence formation	Sentence structure
19	B	Syntax	Effective language usage
20	D	Style and tone	Effective language usage
21	A	Support	Development
22	D	Introduction/conclusion/ transition	Organization

Writing Workout C

1   C   The sentence refers to all of the readers and includes the author in its point of view. In the first part of the sentence, the author writes, "Weekends, like many parts of our lives…" For the sake of consistency, use *we* to match *our*. The term *American workers* is not possessive but inclusive.

2   D   The sentence requires the present tense verb *relies*. (The Saturday-Sunday weekend is a current reality.) The verb *relies* best fits with the preposition *on*. The phrase *relies for* (B) is not idiomatic English.

3   D   All of the choices can express a sense of production, creation, or bringing into existence. However, *compounded* (A) is usually used in the sense of putting physical objects together to make something new (*the pharmacist compounded a prescription drug*, for example). *Caused* (B) is awkward in this context. The weekend was *established* (D) by a process of social and legal change.

4   A   In this case, commas are needed to separate the items in the series; the sentence is fine as is. Using a single semicolon (B) or a colon (C) in a simple list that already is separated by commas is inconsistent use of punctuation. Choice B also is missing *in*, making the parenthetical phrase not parallel with the others in the sentence. D is missing the comma required to separate items in the list.

5   D   Choice D is correct because the plural of *Sunday* is created by simply adding *s*; adding an apostrophe-*s* creates a possessive, which isn't the type of word needed here. Choice B is incorrect because it moves the comma from after *playing* to before *playing*.

6   B   The underlined part as it appears is a bit awkward. If you notice that horse races and cricket matches are examples of sporting events, you can see how the sentence should be worded. Mentioning horse races and cricket matches adds detail, but horse races and cricket matches aren't grammatically necessary to the structure and meaning of the sentence; they can be set off by commas.

7   A   Without the reference to "Saint Monday" in paragraph 3, the reference to it in the next sentence comes out of nowhere and will confuse the reader.

8   B   A clue to the correct answer appears later in this sentence. The phrase *showing up for work* makes the use of *working* or *workers* in the underlined portion redundant. It's enough to say that the number of people showing up for work was too small.

9   D   Sentences 2 and 3 in paragraph 5 describe a cause-and-effect relationship, which is correctly signaled by the transition word *consequently*: As a consequence of the small number of people showing up for work, owners cut the length of the work week. *On the other hand* (A) signals a contrast; *in fact* (B) sets up an example; *furthermore* (C) signals a continuation.

10 C   Sentence 5 describes a factory that's been idled because it has no workers. Of the four possible placements, sentence 5 fits best after sentence 2, which states that factories had to shut down when people failed to show up for work. Sentence 5 elaborates on this idea.

11 A Choices C and D are unnecessarily wordy. Choice B makes it sound like workers demanded a five-day workweek because Congress passed the Fair Labor Standards Act, which doesn't make sense. Combining the sentences with a semicolon makes the simplest, clearest sentence.

12 B Choices A and D are a bit too casual for an essay of this type. *Alone* (B), which is an adjective describing weight, is a better fit than *itself*, which is a pronoun used for emphasis.

13 C The sentence does not fit at this point because it neither relates to the main idea of the paragraph nor leads into the next paragraph. The sentence might fit better later in the passage, once the obesity problem and its worldwide nature are established. But at this point, the direction of the passage as a whole hasn't become clear yet, so that's not the place for a very broad statement about the need for a serious fight against overweight and obesity.

14 B The pronoun in the underlined portion refers to the singular noun *person*, so a singular pronoun is needed here. Using either *he* or *she* alone would be grammatically correct, but *he or she* is the best choice to include both genders. When used together like this, *he or she* takes the singular form of the verb: *he or she weighs*.

15 D The sentence as it appears is a fragment. Deleting the underlined portion fixes the problem.

16 C The graph shows precise figures for the percentage of North American men (30 percent) and women (33 percent) who are obese, so choice C is the most accurate. "A full third" (A) is not quite precise enough. Choice B is incorrect because the percentage-point increases for both Asia and Latin America were greater. The passage defines the difference between obesity and overweight, and there's no way to know if choice D is accurate because the chart deals only with obesity.

17 A The paragraph is about the prevalence of overweight and obesity around the world, and choice A offers an illustrating detail about its impact. Choice A also follows naturally from the preceding sentence, which raises the topic of diabetes.. The information in choice B is already implied within this paragraph and the preceding paragraph, so it isn't needed here. Choices C and D are not relevant to this paragraph.

18 C The sentence discusses the potential for improvement in rates of obesity, overweight, and diabetes in the future ("the next several years"), so the future tense is required.

19 B The sentence as it appears is a run-on. Choice C creates a comma splice. Choice D adds the conjunction *but*, signaling a reversal in logic that doesn't exist between the two clauses. Choice B breaks the run-on into two grammatically correct sentences.

20 A One usage of *while* is as a conjunction meaning *at the same time*. Substitute *at the same time* in place of *while*, and the exact relationship between *on-course* and *off-course* in the report is very clear. *Because* (B) implies a cause-and-effect relationship that doesn't exist. *More so* (C) means *to a greater degree*, which doesn't express the correct relationship either.

21 B *Lousy zero* (A) is too casual for a formal essay of this type, as are choices C and D. The best bet here is to go with the shortest choice.

22 A The paragraph fits best where it is because it continues the introductory description of BMI that began in the first paragraph.

Writing Workout C Item Breakout

ITEM	KEY	SKILL	CONTENT DIMENSION
1	C	Pronouns	Usage
2	D	Conventional Expression	Usage
3	D	Precision	Effective language use
4	A	Items in a series	Punctuation
5	D	Frequently confused words	Usage
6	B	Items in a series	Punctuation
7	A	Support	Development
8	B	Concision	Effective language use
9	D	Introduction/conclusion/transition	Organization
10	C	Logical sequence	Organization
11	A	Sentence formation	Sentence structure
12	B	Style and tone	Effective language use
13	C	Introduction/conclusion/transition	Organization
14	B	Agreement	Usage
15	D	Sentence formation	Sentence structure
16	C	Quantitative information	Development
17	A	Support	Development
18	C	Shift in construction	Sentence structure
19	B	End-of-sentence punctuation	Punctuation
20	A	Precision	Effective language use
21	B	Style and tone	Effective language use
22	A	Logical sequence	Organization

Writing Workout D

1   C   *Meet* and *gather* mean about the same thing. *Buying* and *selling* are implied in the word *shop*. Using them all in the same sentence is redundant. Choice C eliminates the redundancies.

2   B   The project began in the past (2009), continues in the present, and may continue into the future. This requires the present perfect tense: *have been* plus the present participle of *fund* to create *have been funding*.

3   C   *Sight* (used as a noun, choice A) refers to something that is seen. A place or a location is a *site*. The word *cite* (choice B) means *to refer to* something. The word *slight* (choice D) means *a small amount*.

4   B   The sentence as it appears doesn't make sense because we don't know who *they* are. Choice B clarifies this and arranges the clauses in the proper time order: The restoration project started turning up artifacts, so archaeologists were called in. Choice C doesn't work because the restoration project was started before the archeologists were called in, not when they were called in. Choice D is a sentence fragment.

5   A   The phrase *In all* makes the best transition from the statement that the bog was full of tools to the exact number that were catalogued. *On the other hand* (B) and *nonetheless* (C) hint that a contradiction is coming next, but that is not the case. The phrase *for instance* (D) suggests it will be followed by one or more examples of the kind of tools found, but examples have already been given.

6   B   The sentence as it appears is off-topic for the paragraph. Choice B confirms the ancient nature of the Redmond find. Choice D is incorrect because *several decades ago*, while it seems like a long time in terms of a human life span, is not correctly considered *ancient*.

7   D   As written, the paragraph is disjointed. It starts by mentioning glaciers, leaving the reader to wonder, *What glaciers? Where did that come from?* The only choice that brings together the two sentences that discuss glaciers is choice D. Sentence 5 introduces the idea of glaciers, and sentence 1 (moved to follow sentence 5) expands on the idea that glaciers have reshaped the landscape.

8   D   Choice A misplaces the modifier *Like the mall that stands nearby*. We aren't quite sure exactly what is being compared to the mall. Choice B combines the past and the present in a way that doesn't make much sense, plus it uses the wrong form of the verb (*indicates* instead of *indicate*).

Choice C also doesn't make much sense, and the text that follows the semicolon is not an independent clause. Choice D combines the sentences clearly, showing that the site was a gathering place in ancient times, somewhat like the mall is a gathering place today.

9   A   *Who* refers to a subject and *whom* refers to an object. The subject is the one doing something, and the object is the one having something done to it. The Muckleshoot and Snoqualmie people are the ones enjoying salmon, deer, and the other animals. They're the ones who are doing something. Therefore, the proper pronoun to use is *who*. *That* (choice D) (as opposed to *which*) is incorrect because it's the wrong pronoun to use in a nonrestrictive clause. In addition, *that* is not the correct pronoun to use when referring to people.

10 A The paragraph goes into great detail about the ancient tools and their importance. Although the sentence contrasts with the one that precedes it, the information it contains is irrelevant to the paragraph.

11 D No punctuation is needed here.

12 C This passage is a formal, descriptive essay. The sentence uses an inappropriately casual tone for such an essay. It also unnecessarily injects the author (*I*) into an essay in which he or she otherwise does not appear.

13 A The first two sentences in this paragraph say that computers don't usually deal in probabilities, only exact calculations. This third sentence introduces a contrasting idea: that probabilistic programming languages offer a way for computers to deal with inexact (probabilistic) calculations. The word *however* signals that this sentence is in opposition to the previous two.

14 D The paragraph says that introduction of probabilistic programming methods has led to an extensive body of work in machine learning, etcetera, and discoveries continue up to the present time. The ongoing expansion of the body of work requires the present perfect tense, *has given*.

15 C Items in series are separated by commas. Choice C does so correctly. Choice D omits the comma after *neuroscience*.

16 B The subject of the sentence is *discoveries*, which requires the plural verb *continue*. The plural noun *developments* requires the plural pronoun *these*.

17 C The paragraph describes Galileo's method of enumerating probabilities. Choice C makes the first sentence of the paragraph an effective topic sentence.

18 D *Alternative* and *different* have similar meanings—anything that is an alternative would be different. Using both is redundant. The most concise choice that eliminates the redundancy is D.

19 A The diagram shows a continuous process in which input leads to output, then output immediately becomes input for further analysis. In other words, the analysis runs both forward from causes (input) to effects (data) and backward from effects (data) to causes. The passage makes clear that probabilistic models can determine the likelihood of certain events (B) and that data is used in such programs (C). Nothing in the passage supports the idea that it ensures correct decisions, however (D).

20 B When referring to a college degree, *bachelor's* is structured as a singular possessive, with apostrophe + *s*. It's important to pay close attention to possessives.

21 B The underlined portion is too casual for an essay of this type, as is choice C. Deleting the underlined portion takes out information that's necessary. The sentence would read, "An important criterion is working well because programming often requires such collaboration" which leaves the reader wondering "working well on what, or with whom?"

22 D The work has two requirements: attention to detail and knowledge of programming languages. To maintain parallel structure, both requirements must be handled in the same way. The verb *having* is unnecessary.

Writing Workout D Item Breakout

ITEM	KEY	SKILL	CONTENT DIMENSION
1	C	Items in a series	Punctuation
2	B	Shift in construction	Sentence structure
3	C	Frequently confused words	Usage
4	B	Sentence formation	Sentence structure
5	A	Introduction, conclusion, transition	Organization
6	B	Support	Development
7	D	Logical sequence	Organization
8	D	Concision	Effective language use
9	A	Pronouns	Usage
10	A	Support	Development
11	D	Within-sentence punctuation	Punctuation
12	C	Style and tone	Effective language use
13	A	Introduction/conclusion/transition	Organization
14	D	Agreement	Usage
15	C	Items in a series	Punctuation
16	B	Precision	Effective language use
17	C	Support	Development
18	D	Concision	Effective language use
19	A	Quantitative information	Development
20	B	Possessive nouns and pronouns	Punctuation
21	B	Style and tone	Effective language use
22	D	Concision	Effective language use

Writing Workout E

1 **A** Vessels travel on inland waterways. The simple possessive (A) is correct. Choice B is the right form of a possessive, but the wrong word.

2 **D** *Insure* (A) means "to get financial protection," as in an insurance policy. *Assure* (B) means "to say everything is OK." *Ensure* means "to make certain," which is the idea that's needed here. To *affirm* (C) is to assert that something is true. It could be made to fit in this case, but *ensure* is a stronger choice. Always choose the best option, not one that's just good enough.

3 **B** *Transport* and *carry* mean the same thing, so there's no need to use both. Choice B eliminates the redundancy.

4 **A** Coal and iron ore are specific examples of heavy commodities. The other choices are too general and don't really tell the reader more than *heavy commodities* has already said.

5 **D** The underlined portion is off topic. It has nothing to do with the rest of the paragraph, which is listing the different tasks of water transportation workers. It's logical to assume such workers would have to know how to swim, but this isn't the right spot to discuss their qualifications.

6 **C** No punctuation is necessary here. A colon (A) can be used to introduce a list, such as the list of those employed on a large ship, but the part of the sentence following the colon isn't structured properly for that.

7 **D** The sentence is specific about the number of mates and assistant engineers on a large shop, but is not specific about how many sailors and marine oilers are aboard. Of the choices given, the best way to express this non-specific figure is to say *several*. The word *amount* is used to indicate mass or a quantity that isn't easily counted. The word *number* would work better here—sailors and marine oilers can be counted—but it's not given as an option.

8 **B** The sentence contradicts the one before it. Large ships have large crews; smaller vessels may have smaller crews. *However* is the best choice to signal the contradiction.

9 **D** The paragraph discusses the function of mates after explaining the function of captains, so the sentence does not belong at the beginning of the paragraph.

10 **C** The sentence as it appears is awkward, so choice A can't be right. Choice B doesn't make sense. At this point in the paragraph, the context indicates that we're talking about what captains do, so choice D won't fit. Choice C is the last one left. It has the right reference for *they* (the noun *captains*) and puts the prepositional phrases in the right places for the sentence to be clear.

11 **A** Choice A joins the two sentences without creating any new grammatical errors. Choice B creates a run-on sentence, and choice C creates a comma splice. If the two sentences were combined as in choice D, parallel structure would require the second verb (*help*) to be structured in the same way as the first verb in the new sentence (*work*), so *helping* (D) is the wrong form.

12 D Each choice expresses the sense that panda preservation is a highly valuable activity. *Awesome* (A) is too casual, however. The words *grand* (B) and *remarkable* (C) can both have the sense of *impressive* or *extraordinary*, but neither fits with the tone and purpose of the passage. Choice D, *important*, has precisely the right sense and is appropriate.

13 C The referent of the underlined pronoun *they* is unclear. Choice C fixes this problem: *pandas live* in the region that overlaps with many other species found only in China.

14 A Only choice A correctly describes the relationships of the species shown in the diagram.

15 D The names of the two researchers, Stuart Pimm and Binbin Li, make up a nonrestrictive element. Their names could be removed from the sentence without the sentence losing its meaning. Nonrestrictive elements are set off by commas, parentheses, or dashes as appropriate.

16 C Each item in a series is followed by a comma. No comma is necessary following the last item (B). The word *and* is necessary before the final item in a series of more than two, so choice D can't be right. Whether to use a serial comma—a comma preceding the final item in a series—is an editorial choice that won't be tested on the PSAT or SAT. You'll note that eliminating the serial comma is not an option for this question.

17 B The paragraph describes the sequence of events in the making of the Duke University study. Pimm and Li created a database, used it to create a new map, and finally matched their new map with existing maps. None of the other choices make the sequence clear. Choices C and D also don't really fit with the logic and meaning of the rest of the sentence and paragraph.

18 A If sentence 2 is moved, it's not clear to the reader where the database discussed in sentence 3 comes from. It should stay where it is now.

19 B Some areas are completely unprotected. Others have lesser degrees of protection. Both of these situations exist at the same time. *While* best expresses that relationship.

20 C The "immediate impact" mentioned in the first sentence suggests that the Chinese government will move quickly.

21 B *Eminent* (A) means *famous* or *respected*, which makes no sense in this context. *Imminent* (B) means "about to happen," which is the meaning needed here. *Intimate* means *close*, but in the sense of personal relationships and not proximity. *Permanent* could be correct if the destruction had already taken place, but the rest of the paragraph indicates that the Chinese government was able to force the railroad to reroute so that it wouldn't harm the panda habitat.

22 C The subject of the sentence is *recommendations*, a plural word, which requires the verb *protect*, not *protects* (A, D). The better protection referred to has yet to happen, however, so the sentence requires the future tense.

Writing Workout E Item Breakout

ITEM	KEY	SKILL	CONTENT DIMENSION
1	A	Frequently confused words	Usage
2	D	Frequently confused words	Usage
3	B	Concision	Effective language use
4	A	Precision	Effective language use
5	D	Focus	Development
6	C	Within-sentence punctuation	Punctuation
7	D	Conventional expression	Usage
8	B	Introduction/conclusion/transition	Organization
9	D	Proposition	Development
10	C	Syntax	Effective language use
11	A	Sentence formation	Sentence structure
12	D	Style and tone	Effective language use
13	C	Pronouns	Usage
14	A	Support	Development
15	D	Nonrestrictive and parenthetical elements	Punctuation
16	C	Items in a series	Punctuation
17	B	Introduction/conclusion/transition	Organization
18	A	Logical sequence	Organization
19	B	Sentence formation	Sentence structure
20	C	Support	Development
21	B	Frequently confused words	Usage
22	C	Agreement	Usage

Writing Workout F

1   **D**   The author sets up a pattern in the sentence using the phrase "so much." To maintain the pattern, the end of the sentence should read "so much warmer in winter!" The two phrases ("so much cooler in summer" and "so much warmer in winter") are in parallel structure.

2   **A**   Choice B is a comma splice. Choice C is in passive voice. Choice D is awkward and doesn't make much sense. Choice A joins the two sentences in a grammatically correct sentence.

3   **B**   The two things done by the bee in this sentence, expressed by verbs, must be constructed in the same way: *she prefers* and *she dislikes* (B).

4   **D**   The extra clause makes the whole sentence awkward. It's unnecessary and somewhat redundant, and it can be deleted. Choice B is inappropriate for the tone of the passage. Choice C introduces a redundancy (*trick* and *tricks*).

5   **C**   Choices A, B, and D don't make sense in the context. Choice C accurately expresses the sense that, if the bees suspected what the bee-hunter was doing, they could baffle him by taking a circuitous route.

6   **A**   The sentence as it appears makes an effective transition between the previous sentence ("can be imposed upon by any novice") and the information that follows, about how it takes experience and skill to find a bee tree.

7   **B**   What is the sportsman tracking—his retreat, his dog, or his game? He's tracking his game, so *game* needs to be placed nearer to the verb *track* to make this clear. For that reason, choices A and D can't be right. Where is the hunter tracking the game? He's tracking his game to its retreat, or the place where it lives. Choice B makes this most clear.

8   **C**   Because there's only one task, use the singular form of the verb, *is*. The other three choices use the plural form of the verb, *are*, and can be ZAPPED.

9   **A**   The paragraph explains that a successful bee-hunter needs skills that are sharpened by practice. The author says that after a while he saw and heard bees wherever he went—even when he was standing on a busy city street corner, and pedestrians near him were oblivious to the bees. The detail offers support for the the main idea of the paragraph, which is that training is required in order to notice bees (and find a bee-tree).

10   **C**   Honey ("great nuggets and wedges of precious ore") is stored by the bees somewhere in the woods. It has been *gathered* (C) with risk and labor from fields and woods.

11   **A**   The main argument of the passage is that understanding the ways of bees and how to hunt them are special skills that develop over time. Choice A best summarizes this argument. Choices B and D contradict the main argument. Choice C restates a detail from the first paragraph.

12   C   The paragraph sets up a contrast between "ordinary cloud cover" and the darkness on this particular day. The darkness was not ordinary cloud cover. It was like the falling of night. The only choice that makes the contrast clear is *Instead*.

13   A   The part of a flower that opens and closes is a *petal*. A *pedal* is a foot-operated lever of the kind found on a bicycle or a piano.

14   B   A colon can be used to introduce a quotation. A comma would be also be correct in this spot, although we're not given that option in the answer choices. Some experts recommend using a colon to introduce long quotations such as this one.

15   B   The sun and the moon always have colors of some sort, so this sentence is vague at best. (So are choices C and D.) Choice B offers the most precise description of the "strange" colors of the sun and moon on this night.

16   D   The phrase *who was camped in New Jersey with the Continental Army* is a nonrestrictive or parenthetical phrase. If it's removed from the sentence, the sentence will still be grammatically correct. Such phrases are set off by commas. Choices B and C add unnecessary commas.

17   C   The author has already established that the dark day took place in 1780. The date of Dwight's birth is not important or necessary to the discussion of the dark day.

18   D   No pronoun is needed. The irreligious spent the day in taverns.

19   A   Broadcasting and the Internet are examples of mass communication and are implied in the phrase, so there's no need to repeat them. A comma is needed after communication (A), making B incorrect.

20   B   The sentence as it appears is a fragment. It has no subject. Choice B gives the sentence a subject (*the darkness*) and creates an adverbial phrase with *as* to describe how and/or when the darkness descended. Choice C simply adds an unnecessary comma without correcting the fragment. Choice D is awkward and does not correct the fragment.

21   C   A semicolon is the best of the options for joining the two clauses, both of which can stand alone as complete sentences. Choice B creates a comma splice. Choice D creates a run-on.

22   D   Sentence 3 discusses the sunrise on the next day, so it should follow all of the details of the dark day and appear at the very end of the paragraph.

Writing Workout F Item Breakout

ITEM	KEY	SKILL	CONTENT DIMENSION
1	D	Sentence formation	Sentence structure
2	A	Sentence formation	Sentence structure
3	B	Inappropriate shift in construction	Sentence structure
4	D	Concision	Effective language use
5	C	Introduction/conclusion/transition	Organization
6	A	Introduction/conclusion/transition	Organization
7	B	Syntax	Effective language use
8	C	Possessive determiners	Usage
9	A	Support	Development
10	C	Inappropriate shift in construction	Sentence structure
11	A	Proposition	Development
12	C	Introduction/conclusion/transition	Organization
13	A	Frequently confused words	Usage
14	B	Within-sentence punctuation	Punctuation
15	B	Precision	Effective language use
16	D	Nonrestrictive/parenthetical elements	Punctuation
17	C	Focus	Development
18	D	Pronouns	Usage
19	A	Concision	Effective language use
20	B	Syntax	Effective language use
21	C	Within-sentence punctuation	Punctuation
22	D	Introduction/conclusion/transition	Organization

Math Workout A: No Calculator

1 D The unknown value in the expression is the number of miles from the airport to the hotel. For each mile, the trip will cost $1.95, so you must multiply the number of miles by 1.95. In addition to the cost per mile, the taxi service charges a fee of $5 for every trip. This amount is the same for every trip, no matter the distance. The expression *$1.95 times the number of miles, plus $5* can be written as $1.95x + 5$. Since, the family has less than 6 members, the number of family members is irrelevant..

2 B You can use factoring or the quadratic formula to find the value of x.

Rewrite the equation as $x^2 + 9x - 70 = 0$. Then find the possible values of x:
$(x + 14)(x - 5) = 0$, so $x = -14$ or $x = 5$.

Remember that the quadratic formula is $x = \dfrac{-b \pm \sqrt{b^2 - 4ac}}{2a}$ when your equation takes the form $ax^2 + bx + c = 0$.

In this case, $a = 1$, $b = 9$, and $c = -70$. Substitute these values into the formula and simplify:

$$x = \frac{-9 \pm \sqrt{9^2 - 4(1)(-70)}}{2(1)} = \frac{-9 \pm \sqrt{81 + 280}}{2} = \frac{-9 \pm \sqrt{361}}{2} = \frac{-9 \pm 19}{2}$$

So, $x = \dfrac{-9 + 19}{2} = \dfrac{10}{2} = 5$ OR $x = \dfrac{-9 - 19}{2} = \dfrac{-28}{2} = -14$

The problem tells you that $x < 0$, so x must be -14.

The problem asks for $x + 6$, so $-14 + 6 = -8$.

3 B First solve the system of equations. You can combine like terms in the first equation, then multiply both sides of the equation by 2. This allows you eliminate the y terms when you add the two equations:

$7x + 3y = 5x - 4$
$3x - 6y = -13$

$2x + 3y = -4$ (Combine like terms.)
$3x - 6y = -13$

$4x + 6y = -8$ (Multiply top equation by 2.)
$3x - 6y = -13$

   $7x = -21$ (Add the two equations.)
    $x = -3$

Substitute the value of x into one of the equations to find y.

$3(-3) - 6y = -13$
   $-9 - 6y = -13$
      $-6y = -4$
        $y = \dfrac{2}{3}$

Now find the value of $\dfrac{x}{y}$. Remember when you divide by a fraction, you multiply by its reciprocal.

$$-3 \div \frac{2}{3} = -3 \times \frac{3}{2} = -\frac{9}{2}$$

4 D Evie's two brothers each move the same number of bricks. If you multiply the number that each brother carries by 2 and add that to the number of bricks Evie carries, you get the total, which is 975. In the equation, x represents the number of bricks that each brother moves, and y represents the number of bricks that Evie carries.

5 A Together, the hoses can drain the pool in 2 hours. In the equation, $\frac{1}{2}$ represents the fraction of the pool that the two hoses could drain together in 1 hour. Each term on the left side of the equation represents the part of the $\frac{1}{2}$ that one of the hoses could drain during that 1 hour. The faster hose can drain three times faster than the slower hose, so $\frac{3}{p}$ represents the amount that the faster hose can drain in 1 hour.

6 C Use the distributive property. Simplify each term.

$$\left(\frac{h}{g}\right)(g + h) = \frac{hg}{g} + \frac{h^2}{g} = h + \frac{h^2}{g}$$

7 A Multiply the terms. Remember that $i^2 = -1$

$(9i - 4)(5i + 6)$

$= 45i^2 + 54i - 20i - 24$
$= 45i^2 + 34i - 24$
$= -45 + 34i - 24$
$= -69 + 34i$

8 C This type of problem is sometimes called a compound inequality. You can solve it the same way you solve a regular inequality, by getting the variable by itself. You'll want to get x by itself in the middle part of the inequality.

$45 > 6x + 15 > 27$

Subtract 15 from each part. Then divide each part by 6.

$45 - 15 > 6x + 15 - 15 > 27 - 15$
$30 > 6x > 12$
$30 \div 6 > 6x \div 6 > 12 \div 6$
$5 > x > 2$

So: $17 > 2x + 7 > 11$ (Multiply by 2 and add 7.)

C is the only answer choice between 11 and 17.

9 9

Simplify, then solve for t.

$$\frac{17 + (t - 27)}{3} = \frac{-2t + 15}{9}$$

$$\frac{-10 + t}{3} = \frac{-2t + 15}{9}$$

$$9(-10 + t) = 3(-2t + 15)$$

$$-90 + 9t = -6t + 45$$

$$15t = 135$$

$$t = 9$$

10 4

Multiply the terms.

$$(x - 9)(x + c) = x^2 + cx - 9x - 9c$$

You can write this as $x^2 + (c - 9)x - 9c$.

If you set this equal to the known product, $x^2 - 5x - 36$, you know that the coefficients of like terms from the two expressions must be equal.

$$c - 9 = -5$$

$$9c = 36$$

Solving either of these equations shows that $c = 4$.

Math Workout A: No Calculator Item Breakout

ITEM	KEY	SKILL	CONTENT DIMENSION
1	D	Heart of Algebra	Create, solve, or interpret linear equations in one variable
2	B	Passport to Advanced Math	Solve a quadratic equation
3	B	Heart of Algebra	Algebraically solve systems of two linear equations in two variables
4	D	Heart of Algebra	Interpret the variables and constants in expressions for linear functions within the context presented
5	A	Passport to Advanced Math	Interpret parts of nonlinear expressions in terms of their context
6	C	Passport to Advanced Math	Determine the most suitable form of an expression
7	A	Additional Topics in Math	Add, subtract, multiply, divide, and simplify complex numbers
8	C	Heart of Algebra	Create, solve, or interpret linear inequalities in one variable
9	9	Heart of Algebra	Algebraically solve linear equations or inequalities in one variable
10	4	Passport to Advanced Math	Add, subtract, and multiply polynomial expressions

Math Workout A: Calculator Permitted

1 **B** First determine the miles driven by multiplying the average speed *x* hours. Then divide miles driven by the rate of fuel consumption to determine the gallons consumed.

Doug:
$$F = \frac{60(3.5)}{31} = 6.78 \text{ gallons}$$

Dwight:
$$F = \frac{72(2.75)}{28} = 7.07 \text{ gallons}$$

Marcel:
$$F = \frac{45(6.25)}{44} = 6.40 \text{ gallons}$$

Oliver:
$$F = \frac{50(2)}{15} = 6.68 \text{ gallons}$$

Dwight used the most fuel.

2 **B** You need to create two equations, each with the variables *c* and *a*, to solve this problem. If *c* is the number of child tickets and *a* is the number of adult tickets, then their sum is the total number of tickets, which is 629. The first equation is $c + a = 629$.

You know that a child ticket sells for $5.50, and that the museum sold *c* child tickets. The total price for these tickets is 5.5*c*. You know that an adult ticket sells for $11, and that the museum sold *a* adult tickets. The total price for these tickets is 11*a*. The total price for all the tickets is $5,027. The second equation is $5.5c + 11a = 5,027$.

3 **B** To find the average number of students per teacher, find approximate values for number of students and number of teachers at a point along the line of best fit. Then divide to find the number of students per teacher. You may want to choose approximate values at two different points to make sure your answer is correct.

For example, you could put a point on the line that is very close to 1,000 students and 45 teachers. When you divide 1,000 by 45, you see that there are about 22.2 students for every teacher.

You could choose a second point to check your work at about 1,400 students and about 62 teachers. When you divide 1,400 by 62, you see that there are about 22.6 students per teacher.

The most reasonable answer is 22.

4 D The likelihood that a man will prefer the chicken sandwich is $\frac{78}{168}$ (.4642 or .46). The likelihood that a woman will prefer the chicken sandwich is $\frac{71}{192}$ (.3697 or .37).

Now you can set up an equation. It might be helpful to use words to create your equation:

"The likelihood that a man will prefer the chicken sandwich is y TIMES the likelihood that a woman will prefer the chicken sandwich."

$\frac{78}{168} = y\frac{71}{192}$

$78 \times 192 = 168 \times 71y$ ⠀⠀⠀⠀⠀⠀⠀⠀(Multiply both sides of the equation by 168, and multiply both sides of the equation by 192.)

⠀⠀⠀⠀⠀$y = 1.255533199$, or about 1.26

OR, you can convert the fractions to decimals and work the problem this way:

⠀$.46 = y(.37)$

Divide both sides of the equation by .37.

The answer is 1.24. While this doesn't quite match 1.26 (choice D), that's due to rounding error when converting the fractions $\frac{78}{168}$ and $\frac{71}{192}$ to decimals. Choice D is the correct answer:

According to the survey results, man is about 1.26 times more likely to prefer the chicken sandwich than a woman is.

5 D Based on the survey, 211 of 360 customers prefer the hamburger. To find out how many customers out of 72,000 will prefer the hamburger, you can set up a proportion:

$\frac{211}{360} = \frac{x}{72,000}$

$360x = 211 \cdot 72,000$

$360x = 15,192,000$

⠀$x = 42,200$

6 A There were 71 women surveyed who prefer the chicken sandwich. All together, <u>360 people</u> were surveyed.

$\frac{71}{360} = 0.197222222$, or about 20%

7 D Segment *AF* bisects Segment *BC*. Segment *AF* also bisects Angle *BAC* because Triangle *AGD* is similar to Triangle *AFC*. This means that Angle *FAC* is half of Angle *BAC*, which is 105°. Angle *FAC* is 105 ÷ 2 = 52.5°.

The sum of the measures of the interior angles of a triangle are 180°. You know the measures of two of the angles of Triangle *AGE*. Subtract their sum to find the measure of the third angle. 180 − (52.5 + 90) = 37.5°.

The sum of the measures of two angles that make a straight line is 180°. Angle *AEG* and Angle *GEC* make a straight line. 180 − 37.5 = 142.5°.

8 A $g(x) = 5x^2 + ax - 14$

Substitute 0 for $g(x)$. Substitute $\frac{7}{5}$ for x. Solve for a.

$$0 = 5\left(\frac{7}{5}\right)^2 + \frac{7}{5}a - 14$$

$$0 = 5\left(\frac{49}{25}\right) + \frac{7}{5}a - 14$$

$$0 = \frac{49}{5} + \frac{7}{5}a - 14$$

$$0 = 49 + 7a - 70$$

$$0 = 7a - 21$$

$$21 = 7a$$

$$3 = a$$

9 A $y \geq -\frac{4}{3}x + 3$.

The solution set of $y < x + 5$ is the shaded area in Figure 1. The solution set of $-3y \leq 4x - 9$ is the shaded area in Figure 2. The only section that is part of both solution sets is the shaded area in Figure 3, which is choice A.

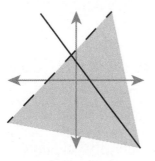

Figure 1

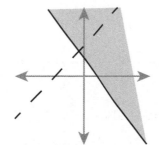

Figure 2

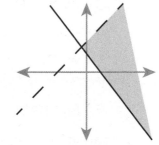

Figure 3

10 B The association between the variables is positive, because as the value of one variable increases, the value of the other variable also increases. The data cannot be represented by a line of best fit, so you know that the association is not linear.

11 **C** You can solve this by setting the two equivalent forms equal to each other and isolating Z on one side of the equation.

$$\frac{9x^2 + 6x}{3x + 7} = \frac{35}{3x + 7} + Z$$

$$Z = \frac{9x^2 + 6x}{3x + 7} - \frac{35}{3x + 7}$$

$$Z = \frac{9x^2 + 6x - 35}{3x + 7}$$

Now you can factor the numerator.

$$Z = \frac{(3x + 7)(3x - 5)}{3x + 7}$$

$$Z = 3x - 5$$

12 **A** The quickest way to solve this is to substitute a number for a and solve for y. You know that $a < -1$, so you can use $a = -2$.

$$y + 3 = -2(x - y)$$
$$y + 3 = -2x + 2y$$
$$y - 2y = -2x - 3$$
$$-y = -2x - 3$$
$$y = 2x + 3$$

This matches the graph of choice A.

Using $a = -2$ gets you a possible linear equation. It's important to recognize that there are other possible answers, because a can equal any number less than -1. But all the answers will have two things in common: The slope and the y-intercept will both be positive.

13 **D** The simplest way of doing this problem is to substitute the ordered pairs and determine which ordered pair satisfies both equations.

14 **C** Substitute $3x$ for y in the first equation, then solve for x^2. Be sure you don't accidentally solve for x.

$$5x^2 - 3(3x)^2 = -198$$
$$5x^2 - 3(9x^2) = -198$$
$$5x^2 - 27x^2 = -198$$
$$-22x^2 = -198$$
$$x^2 = 9$$

15 **C** Logan's aunt will donate $7.50 no matter how far he runs, so that number is a constant. To represent how much she will donate based on how many miles Logan runs, you must multiply the amount per mile ($1.25) by the number of miles (m). To find the total amount of the donation, add the amount Logan's aunt will donate based on how far he runs to the amount she will donate no matter how far he runs.

$$F(m) = 1.25m + 7.5$$

16 A Jasmine has 250 5-ounce bags of marbles. This means that she has 1,250 ounces of marbles. To convert ounces to pounds, divide by 16. Jasmine has $1{,}250 \div 16 = 78.125$ pounds of marbles.

Each box holds 20 pounds of marbles. Divide to find out how many boxes Jasmine needs.

$78.125 \div 20 = 3.90625$

Jasmine needs 4 boxes. The fourth box won't be full.

17 C You need to find the volume of the shorter cylinder, then subtract the volume of the part of the taller cylinder that is inside the shorter cylinder. This will give you the volume of the shorter cylinder that remains for ice.

Volume of a cylinder is the area of the base (the round face) times the height. The area of a circle is $A = \pi r^2$.

The volume of the shorter cylinder is $18 \times \pi \times 9^2 = 1{,}458\pi$ cubic inches.

You only need to find the part of the taller cylinder that is inside the shorter cylinder, so you can use a height of 18 inches.

The volume of the part of the taller cylinder that is inside the larger cylinder is $18 \times \pi \times 6^2 = 648\pi$ cubic inches.

$1{,}458\pi - 648\pi = 810\pi$, or about 2,545 cubic inches.

18 12

You can solve this by setting up a system of two equations. In the first equation, let x be the number of 4-person tables and y be the number of 6-person tables. In the second equation, let x be the number of people sitting at 4-person tables and y be the number of people sitting at 6-person tables.

$$x + y = 40$$
$$4x + 6y = 184$$

Solve for y. You could use substitution. Or you could add the equations.

Multiply the first equation by -4 to cancel out the x terms before you add.

$$-4x + -4y = -160$$
$$4x + 6y = 184$$
$$2y = 24$$
$$y = 12$$

There are 12 6-person tables.

19 601 or 600

Range is the difference between the highest and the lowest value in a set of data. In this problem, you aren't given any exact weight, because the data are presented in a histogram. However, the problem asks for the *smallest possible* range. It's possible that all the moose in the 400−599 section of the histogram weigh 599.49 pounds. It's unlikely, but it's *possible*. Similarly, it's *possible* that all the moose in the 1,200 − 1,399 section weigh 1199.50 pounds. In this very unlikely (but definitely *possible*) case, you would have the highest possible lowest value and the lowest possible highest value. That would give you the smallest possible range for the data set: 1199.50 − 599.49 = 600.01 pounds. Rounded, that's 600 pounds. Alternatively, if you assume the lowest possible high value to be 1200 and the highest possible low value to be 599, then the range would be 1200 − 599 = 601. Either answer is acceptable.

20 121

You know that 35% of the moose are in one section and 10% of the moose are in another section. You need to find the number of moose that are not in either of these sections.

35% + 10% = 45% and 100% − 45% = 55%

This means that you need to find 55% of the total number of moose. There are 220 moose, so find 55% of 220.

220 × 0.55 = 121

You can check your answer:

35% of 220 = 220 × 0.35 = 77 and 10% of 220 = 220 × 0.10 = 22
77 + 22 = 99
220 − 99 = 121

Math Workout A: Calculator Permitted Item Breakout

ITEM	KEY	SKILL	CONTENT DIMENSION
1	B	Problem Solving and Data Analysis	Use ratios, rates, proportional relationships, and scale drawings to solve single- and multi-step problems
2	B	Heart of Algebra	Create, solve, and interpret systems of two linear equations in two variables
3	B	Problem Solving and Data Analysis	Use the relationship between two variables to investigate key features of the graph
4	D	Problem Solving and Data Analysis	Use two-way tables to summarize categorical data and relative frequencies, and calculate conditional probability
5	D	Problem Solving and Data Analysis	Make inferences about population parameters based on sample data
6	A	Problem Solving and Data Analysis	Solve single- and multi-step problems involving percentages
7	D	Additional Topics in Math	Use concepts and theorems about congruence and similarity to solve problems about lines, angles, and triangles
8	A	Passport to Advanced Math	Understand the relationship between zeros and factors of polynomials; use it to sketch graphs
9	A	Heart of Algebra	Create, solve, and interpret systems of linear inequalities in two variables
10	B	Problem Solving and Data Analysis	Given a scatterplot, use linear, quadratic, or exponential models to describe how the variables are related
11	C	Passport to Advanced Math	Create an equivalent form of an algebraic expression
12	A	Heart of Algebra	Understand connections between algebraic and graphical representations
13	D	Passport to Advanced Math	Solve a system of equations consisting of one linear and one quadratic equation in two variables
14	C	Passport to Advanced Math	Use structure to isolate or identify a quantity of interest in an expression or isolate a quantity of interest in an equation
15	C	Heart of Algebra	Build a linear function that models a linear relationship between two quantities
16	A	Problem Solving and Data Analysis	Solve single- and multi-step problems involving measurement quantities, units, and unit conversion
17	C	Additional Topics in Math	Solve problems using volume formulas
18	12	Heart of Algebra	Create, solve, and interpret systems of two linear equations in two variables
19	601 or 600	Problem Solving and Data Analysis	Use statistics to investigate measures of center of data and analyze shape, center, and spread
20	121	Problem Solving and Data Analysis	Solve single- and multi-step problems involving percentages

Math Workout B: No Calculator Answer Explanations

1 D There are two geometry facts that you need to know to work this problem. The sum of the three angles in a triangle is 180°, and vertical angles (opposite angles formed by the intersection of two lines) are congruent.

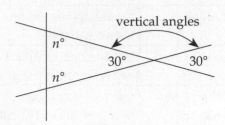

$$n + n + 30 = 180$$
$$n + n = 150$$
$$2n = 150$$
$$n = 75$$

2 C Remember that "When B is subtracted from A" means "A − B." Thus, we're evaluating the expression $(-5 + 2i) - (2 - i)$. Combining like terms, and being careful to distribute the negative, we get $(-5 - 2) + (2i - -i)$, which becomes $-7 + 3i$.

3 B To solve this problem, you need to know the laws of exponents. Remember that $(a^m)(a^n) = a^{m+n}$.

If $a = b^{x+1}$, then:
$ab = (b^{x+1})(b^1) = b^{x+1+1} = b^{x+2}$

4 D To solve this, distribute the negative and combine like terms:

$$(9xy^2 - y^2) - (3x^2y - 5xy^2 - x^2)$$
$$9xy^2 - y^2 - 3x^2y + 5xy^2 + x^2$$
$$(9xy^2 + 5xy^2) - y^2 - 3x^2y + x^2$$
$$14xy^2 - 3x^2y - y^2 + x^2$$

5 A The basic unit of comparison for this problem is the banana, so you need to figure out how many quonks one banana costs. If two bananas cost $6n$ quonks, 1 banana would cost $3n$ quonks. Now you can figure out how many quonks potatoes and loaves of bread cost.

Cost of 1 banana = $3n$ quonks, so:
Cost of 1 potato = $3n + 4$ quonks
Cost of 1 loaf of bread = $(3n + 4) + 4 = 3n + 8$ quonks

Now you must figure out how many quonks it would take to buy 2 loaves of bread and 4 potatoes.

$$2(3n + 8) + 4(3n + 4) = 6n + 16 + 12n + 16$$
$$= 18n + 32 \text{ quonks}$$

6 **C** To find the two solutions, solve the two equations $2x + 1 = 0$ and $x - 3 = 0$. The two solutions are $x = -\frac{1}{2}$ and $x = 3$, respectively.

7 **A** Solve for d in the first equation. Then substitute that value into the second equation and solve for jk.

$\frac{k}{d} = 12$ $jd - 4 = 2$

$d = \frac{k}{12}$ $j\left(\frac{k}{12}\right) = 6$

$\frac{jk}{12} = 6$

$jk = 12 \cdot 6 = 72$

8 **B** Slope $= \dfrac{\text{rise}}{\text{run}} = \dfrac{y_2 - y_1}{x_2 - x_1} = \dfrac{\text{Change in } y}{\text{Change in } x}$

Substitute the coordinates for S and T into this equation to find the value of n.

$\frac{2}{3} = \frac{(n - 2)}{(8 - 2)}$

$\frac{2}{3} = \frac{(n - 2)}{6}$

$\frac{2}{3} \times 6 = (n - 2)$

$4 = n - 2$

$n = 6$

9 79.9

The diameter of a circle passes through its center and is double the radius. The radius of this circle is 40, so its diameter is 80. The greatest length for a segment that does not pass through the center is the greatest number less than the diameter. The greatest number less than 80 that will fit in your grid is 79.9.

10 3

Multiplying both sides of the top equation by 2, we get the system below:
$10x + 14y = 122$
$10x - 3y = 71$

Next, subtracting the bottom equation from the top, we obtain:
$17y = 51$
$y = 3$

Math Workout B: No Calculator Item Breakout

ITEM	KEY	SKILL	CONTENT DIMENSION
1	D	Additional Topics in Math	Use concepts and theorems about congruence and similarity to solve problems about lines, angles, and triangles
2	C	Additional Topics in Math	Add, subtract, multiply, divide, and simplify complex numbers
3	B	Passport to Advanced Math	Create equivalent expressions involving radicals and rational exponents
4	D	Passport to Advanced Math	Add, subtract, and multiply polynomial expressions
5	A	Heart of Algebra	Create, solve, or interpret linear equations in one variable
6	C	Passport to Advanced Math	Solve a quadratic equation
7	A	Passport to Advanced Math	Use structure to isolate or identify a quantity of interest
8	B	Heart of Algebra	Understand connections between algebraic and graphical representations
9	79.9	Additional Topics in Math	Apply theorems about circles to find chord lengths
10	3	Heart of Algebra	Solve systems of two linear equations in two variables

Math Workout B: Calculator Permitted Answer Explanations

1 D This is a multi-step problem. First solve each of the given equations, for m and n respectively, in terms of b.

$$mb + 4 = 9 \qquad nb + 7 = 14$$
$$mb = 9 - 4 \qquad nb = 14 - 7$$
$$mb = 5 \qquad nb = 7$$
$$m = \frac{5}{b} \qquad n = \frac{7}{b}$$

Next solve for $\frac{m}{n}$. Remember that to divide by a fraction, you need to multiply by its reciprocal. This will cancel out the b values and you'll be left with only a fraction.

$$\frac{m}{n} = \frac{\left(\frac{5}{b}\right)}{\left(\frac{7}{b}\right)}$$

$$\frac{m}{n} = \left(\frac{5}{b}\right) \times \left(\frac{b}{7}\right)$$

$$\frac{m}{n} = \frac{5b}{7b}$$

$$\frac{m}{n} = \frac{5}{7}$$

Alternatively:

$$\frac{mb}{nb} = \frac{5}{7}$$
$$\frac{m}{n} = \frac{5}{7}$$

2 A The mean (average) is the total of all the rainfalls divided by the number of rainfalls given:

$$\text{Average} = \frac{\text{total}}{\text{number}} \qquad \frac{(55 + 30 + 35 + 35 + 15 + 40)}{6} = 35 \text{ inches}$$

3 C You can work this problem in two ways. One is a quick process of elimination. You know that $m + n = 10$ and $mn = 16$, so both variables must be positive numbers less than 10. Start by plugging in combinations: $9 + 1 = 10$, but $9 \times 1 = 9$. Doesn't work. $8 + 2 = 10$ and $8 \times 2 = 16$. The values 8 and 2 are correct, so subtract them: $8 - 2 = 6$.

The other way to solve this problem is to solve one of the variables in terms of the other.

$$m + n = 10$$
$$m = 10 - n$$
$$mn = 16$$
$$n(10 - n) = 16$$
$$10n - n^2 - 16 = 0 \qquad \text{Write as a quadratic equation.}$$
$$n^2 - 10n + 16 = 0 \qquad \text{Multiply both sides by } ^-1.$$
$$(n - 8)(n - 2) = 0 \qquad \text{Factor.}$$
$$n - 8 = 0 \quad \text{or} \quad n - 2 = 0 \qquad \text{Set each factor equal to zero.}$$
$$n = 8 \qquad\qquad n = 2$$

If n can be either 8 or 2, then so can m. You can see from the choices that your answer must be positive, so m must be greater than n.

$$m = 8$$
$$n = 2$$
$$m - n = 6$$

4 B Our denominator here is the total number of students who study 3–5 hours per day, and our numerator is the number of the students who study 3–5 hours per day who are also freshmen or sophomores. This is given by $\frac{42}{90}$, which, in lowest terms, is $\frac{7}{15}$.

5 B The total number of students who study between 1 and 5 hours per night, given by the middle two columns, is 162. Out of these 162 students, 41 are juniors. $\frac{41}{162}$ is approximately .25306, which is about 25.3%.

6 D We're given $\dfrac{\frac{(2x - 8)}{7}}{\frac{(10x + 10)}{35}}$. Divide the terms of the denominator by 5:

$$\dfrac{\frac{(2x - 8)}{7}}{\frac{(2x + 2)}{7}}$$

Remembering the rule for fraction division (dividing by a fraction is the same as multiplying by its reciprocal), this becomes:

$$\frac{(2x - 8)}{7} \times \frac{7}{(2x + 2)}$$

Which is just

$$\frac{(2x - 8)}{(2x + 2)}$$

Dividing all terms by 2, we get a final answer of

$$\frac{(x - 4)}{(x + 1)}$$

7 C When the diver hits the water, her height will be 0, meaning $h(d) = 0$. Thus, we need to solve the equation $-d^2 + 2d + 24 = 0$.

This has the same solutions as:
$d^2 - 2d - 24 = 0$

This factors as:
$(d - 6)(d + 4) = 0$

Giving us two solutions: 6 and -4. Since in this context, we can't have a negative answer, our final answer is 6 meters.

8   **A**   Solve for pq in the first equation.

$\frac{5}{pq} = \frac{1}{4}$ (Cross multiply.)

$pq = 20$

Now substitute q^2 for p and solve for q.

$(q^2)q = 20$

$\quad q^3 = 20$

$\quad\; q = \sqrt[3]{20}$

9   **D**   You need to know three formulas to answer this question:

<u>Area of a circle</u> ($A = \pi r^2$) and <u>Area of a rectangle</u> ($A = \text{length} \times \text{width}$).

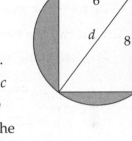

Both are given in the reference information in the test directions. You will also need the <u>Pythagorean theorem</u> ($a^2 + b^2 = c^2$ where c is the hypotenuse, or longest side of a right triangle, and a and b are the other two sides). Begin by drawing a diagonal splitting the rectangle into two triangles. The diagonal is equal to the diameter of the circle, which is two times the radius $\left(r = \frac{d}{2}\right)$.

A right triangle with hypotenuse d and sides 6 and 8 is formed (opposite sides of a rectangle have equal length).

Therefore $6^2 + 8^2 = d^2$	Area of circle $= A = \pi r^2$	Area of rectangle $= A = lw$
$36 + 64 = d^2$	$= \pi \cdot 5^2$	$= 8 \cdot 6$
$100 = d^2$	$= 25\pi$	$= 48$
$10 = d$	Answer: $25\pi - 48$	

Note: It is not necessary to calculate π, as all choices include π as part of the answer.

10   **C**   The fact that the pool is 8 feet deep is extraneous information. You don't need it and you can't use it. The formula for the volume of a rectangular solid is: $V = l \times w \times h$.

You know that the volume is 1170 cubic feet and that $l = 15$ ft. and $w = 12$ ft. Substitute these numbers into the formula to find the depth of the water in the pool (depth can be considered the height of the water).

$\quad V = l \times w \times h$

$1170 = 15 \times 12 \times h$ Multiply length by width.

$1170 = 180 \times h$ Divide 180 on both sides.

$\quad\; h = 6.5$ ft

11   **B**   4 is a local maximum, but not the overall maximum value. Looking in Quadrant II, you can see the function has values greater than 4.

12 A Using the distributive property, we get:
$$3x + 9 < 5x - 3$$

Subtracting 5x from both sides:
$$-2x + 9 < -3$$

Subtracting 9 from both sides:
$$-2x < -12$$

Dividing by -2, and remembering to reverse the inequality sign because we're dividing by a negative number:
$$x > 6$$

Choice B is tempting here, but avoid it. We need an **integer** that's greater than 6. The smallest such integer is 7.

13 C This can be easily answered using exponents. Since the population doubles every 5 years, it will double 10 times in 50 years. To double something is to multiply by 2, so if you take 2 to its tenth power you will have your answer: $2^{10} = 1024$.

14 A The median and mode remain the same (43 and 34, respectively), meaning that the *only* measure of central tendency that changes here is the mean.

15 C The area of a rectangle = length × width. You have all the elements you need to set up an equation to solve for n.

$$A = l \times w$$
$$40 = (n + 3) \times (n - 3)$$
$$40 = n^2 - 9$$
$$40 = n^2 - 9$$
$$49 = n^2$$
$$n = 7$$

Possibly this problem could be solved more quickly by substituting in the choices.

16 B The formula for finding the slope of a line is:

$$\frac{\text{rise}}{\text{run}} \quad \text{or} \quad \frac{y_2 - y_1}{x_2 - x_1}$$

You are dividing the amount of (vertical) change in the y-variable by the amount of (horizontal) change in the x-variable. The given ordered pairs are $(0, g)$ and $(3g, 0)$. It doesn't matter which ordered pair you call (x_1, y_1) and which you call (x_2, y_2). The slope will be the same either way.

$$\text{slope} = \frac{(0 - g)}{(3g - 0)}$$
$$\text{slope} = -\frac{g}{3g}$$
$$\text{slope} = -\frac{1}{3}$$

Note: It's important to know the formula for slope because it doesn't appear on the reference information at the beginning of the test. Also, you can *ZAP* choices C and D because the line has a downward slope, indicating that the slope must be negative.

17 D When two parallel lines are cut by a third line, corresponding angles are congruent. You are told that lines x and y are parallel. Therefore, because they are corresponding angles, $a°$ and $3b°$ are equal. Because $a°$ and $b°$ make a straight line, you know that $a° + b° = 180°$. By substituting $3b°$ for $a°$, you have $3b° + b° = 180°$, or $4b° = 180°$.

$4b° = 180°$ Divide both sides by 4.
$b° = 45°$

You know that $a° = 3b°$ so,

$a° = 3(45)$
$a° = 135°$

18 $\frac{1}{4}$ or $\frac{3}{12}$ or .25

Simplify to get ab alone on one side.

$$\left(\frac{1a}{3}\right)(12b) = 1$$

$$3\left(\frac{1a}{3}\right)(12b) = 1(3)$$ Multiply both sides by 3.

$$a(12b) = 3$$

$$\frac{1}{12}(a)(12b) = 3\left(\frac{1}{12}\right)$$ Multiply both sides by $\frac{1}{12}$.

$$ab = \frac{3}{12} = \frac{1}{4}$$

Alternatively:

$$\frac{1}{3}a(12b) = 1$$

$$\frac{1}{3} \bullet 12ab = 1$$

$$4ab = 1$$

$$ab = \frac{1}{4}$$

19 $\frac{29}{4}$ or 7.25

First solve for n.

$$4n - 9 = \frac{9}{4}$$

$$4n - 4 - 5 = \frac{9}{4}$$

$$4n - 4 = 5 + \frac{9}{4}$$

$$4n - 4 = \frac{20}{4} + \frac{9}{4}$$

$$4n - 4 = \frac{29}{4}$$

20   6

This can be solved using the system of equations below:

$.25q + .01p = 21$
$q + p = 156$

Multiplying the bottom equation by .25, we get:

$.25q + .01p = 21$
$.25q + .25p = 39$

If we then subtract the bottom equation from the top one, we get:

$-.24p = -18$

Giving us $p = 75$.

If she has 75 pennies, she has $156 - 75 = 81$ quarters. Thus, the difference is $81 - 75 = 6$.

Math Workout B: Calculator Permitted Item Breakout

ITEM	KEY	SKILL	CONTENT DIMENSION
1	D	Passport to Advanced Math	Use structure to isolate or identify a quantity of interest
2	A	Data Anal ysis	Use statistics to investigate measures of center of data and analyze shape, center, and spread
3	C	Heart of Algebra	Create, solve, or interpret a linear expression or equation in two variables
4	B	Problem Solving and Data Analysis	Use two-way tables to summarize categorical data and relative frequencies, and calculate conditional probability
5	B	Problem Solving and Data Analysis	Use two-way tables to summarize categorical data and relative frequencies, and calculate conditional probability
6	D	Passport to Advanced Math	Rewrite simple rational expressions
7	C	Passport to Advanced Math	Solve a quadratic equation
8	A	Passport to Advanced Math	Use structure to isolate or identify a quantity of interest
9	D	Additional Topics in Math	Use trigonometric ratios and the Pythagorean Theorem to solve applied problems involving right triangles
10	C	Additional Topics in Math	Solve problems using volume formulas
11	B	Passport to Advanced Math	Use function notation, and interpret statements using function notation
12	A	Heart of Algebra	Create, solve, or interpret linear inequalities in one variable
13	C	Passport to Advanced Math	Create a quadratic or exponential function
14	A	Problem Solving and Data Analysis	Use statistics to investigate measures of center of data and analyze shape, center, and spread
15	C	Passport to Advanced Math	Solve a quadratic equation
16	B	Heart of Algebra	Understand connections between algebraic and graphical representations
17	D	Heart of Algebra	Create, solve, or interpret a linear expression or equation in one variable
18	$\frac{1}{4}$ or $\frac{3}{12}$ or .25	Passport to Advanced Math	Use structure to isolate or identify a quantity of interest
19	$\frac{29}{4}$ or 7.25	Heart of Algebra	Create, solve, or interpret a linear expression or equation in one variable
20	6	Heart of Algebra	Create, solve, or interpret systems of linear equations in two variables

Math Workout C: No Calculator Answer Explanations

1 B Since $\frac{x}{y} = 9$, $x = 9y$. Substituting, we get:

$$15(y - 2) + 12 = 9y$$
$$15y - 30 + 12 = 9y$$
$$15y - 18 = 9y$$
$$-18 = -6y$$
$$y = 3$$

Avoid the trap of picking answer choice D at this point! The question asks for $x + y$. Since $y = 3$ and $x = 9y$, $x = 27$. Thus, $x + y = 30$.

2 D Because the parabola is upside down, it has to have a negative leading coefficient. Thus, choices A and B are out right away. The graph crosses the x-axis at $x = -1$ and $x = 3$, meaning the factors are $(x + 1)(x - 3)$.

3 A Dividing all terms by 3 gives us $x^2 - 6x + 2 = 0$. Since we now have a leading coefficient of 1 and an even linear term (6), we can complete the square:

$$x^2 - 6x = -2$$
$$x^2 - 6x + 9 = 7$$
$$(x - 3)^2 = 7$$
$$x - 3 = \pm\sqrt{7}$$
$$x = 3 \pm\sqrt{7}$$

Or, use the Quadratic formula to solve the problem.

4 B His current mile is $5(60) + 10 = 310$ seconds, and he's reducing his time by 1.5 seconds per week—hence the $310 - 1.5w$ in each answer choice.

His goal is to have a mile time below 4.75 minutes, so we can eliminate choices A and C (wrong inequality sign).

Choices C and D failed to convert 4.75 minutes to seconds. Thus, the answer is B.

5 D Cross multiplication gives us the equation:

$$5(x - y) = 8y$$
$$5x - 5y = 8y$$
$$5x = 13y$$
$$\frac{5x}{y} = 13$$
$$\frac{x}{y} = \frac{13}{5}$$

6 A $B - \frac{A}{2} = (3 - x^2) - \frac{-4x^2 + 8x - 2}{2}$

$\qquad = (3 - x^2) - (-2x^2 + 4x - 1)$

$\qquad = 3 - x^2 + 2x^2 - 4x + 1$

$\qquad = -x^2 + 2x^2 - 4x + 3 + 1$

$\qquad = x^2 - 4x + 4$

7 C $\dfrac{-3 - 7i}{-9 - i}$

$\dfrac{-3 - 7i}{-9 - i} \bullet \dfrac{-9 + i}{-9 + i}$

$\dfrac{27 - 3i + 63i - 7i^2}{81 - 9i + 9i - i^2}$

$\dfrac{34 + 60i}{82}$

$\dfrac{17}{41} + \dfrac{30i}{41}$

8 C Since $cos\,x° = \dfrac{3}{5}$, we have:

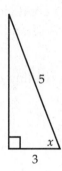

Either recognizing this as a 3-4-5- triangle or using the Pythagorean theorem, the longer leg of the triangle has a length of 4.

Since the actual hypotenuse has a length of 20, we can reason proportionally, as follows:

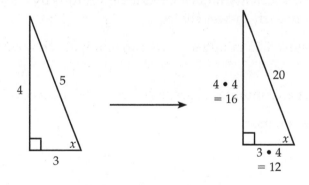

Finally, the area of a triangle is $\dfrac{1}{2}bh$, where b and h are the legs in a right triangle. So our area is $\dfrac{1}{2}(12)(16) = 96$

9   108

We're given: $a = 3\sqrt{3}$ and $4a = \sqrt{4x}$

From the first equation, we have $4a = 12\sqrt{3}$. Thus,

$$12\sqrt{3} = \sqrt{4x}$$
$$\sqrt{(144 \cdot 3)} = \sqrt{4x}$$
$$\sqrt{432} = \sqrt{4x}$$
$$432 = 4x$$
$$x = 108$$

Or, another way is:

$$12\sqrt{3} = \sqrt{4x}$$
$$144 \cdot 3 = 4x$$
$$432 = 4x$$
$$x = 108$$

10   0.7

We're given: $\frac{2}{3}x - \frac{3}{8} = -\frac{29}{120}$

Multiply both sides by 120.

$$80x - 45 = -29$$
$$80x = 16$$
$$x = \frac{16}{80}$$
$$x = \frac{1}{5} \text{ or } .2$$
$$\frac{7x}{2} = \frac{7(0.2)}{2}$$
$$= 7(0.1)$$
$$= 0.7$$

Math Workout C: No Calculator Item Breakout

ITEM	KEY	SKILL	CONTENT DIMENSION
1	B	Heart of Algebra	Solve a system of linear equations
2	D	Passport to Advanced Math	Determine the most suitable form of an expression
3	A	Passport to Advanced Math	Solve a quadratic equation
4	B	Heart of Algebra	Solve linear inequalities
5	D	Problem Solving and Data Analysis	Use ratios, rates, proportional relationships, and scale drawings to solve single- and multi-step problems
6	A	Heart of Algebra	Add, subtract, and multiply polynomial expressions
7	C	Additional Topics in Math	Add, subtract, multiply, divide, and simplify complex numbers
8	C	Passport to Advanced Math	Use the relationship between similarity, right triangles, and trigonometric ratios; use the relationship between sine and cosine of complementary angles
9	108	Passport to Advanced Math	Solve an equation in one variable that contains radicals or contains the variable in the denominator of a fraction
10	0.7	Heart of Algebra	Create, solve, or interpret linear equations in one variable

Math Workout C: Calculator Permitted Answer Explanations

1 **C** Using supplementary angles,

$$(x + 34) + x = 180$$
$$2x + 34 = 180$$
$$2x = 146$$
$$x = 73$$

Angle 1 has measure $x + 34$, so
$m\angle 1 = 107°$

(Use corresponding angles. See the Math Review in this *Study Guide*, beginning on page 61.)

2 **A** Choice A shows a weak positive association. If you sketch a line of best fit, most of the points fall roughly along the line in a positive direction. Choice B shows a negative association. Choice C is random. And Choice D is not a linear association.

3 **B** 4 hours and 33 minutes is $4(60) + 33 = 273$ minutes. Since a sophomore spends 30% more times studying than a freshman, we have:

$$1.3F = S$$
$$1.3F = 273$$
$$F = 210$$

A freshman spends 210 minutes studying, which translates to 3 hours and 30 minutes.

4 **A** The total broadcast time is $2(60) + 15 = 135$ minutes. Of that $\frac{15}{27}$ will not be spent showing commercials, meaning that $\frac{12}{27}$ will be spent showing commercials.

$\frac{12}{27}(135) = 60$, so there are 60 minutes worth of commercials.

If each commercial only lasts 30 seconds (half a minute), there could potentially be

$60 \div 0.5 = 120$ commercials.

If each commercial lasts 45 seconds ($\frac{3}{4}$ of a minute), there would only be

$60 \div 0.75 = 80$ commercials.

Thus, the difference between the maximum number of commercials and the minimum number of commercials is $120 - 80 = 40$.

5 **C** The expression is undefined whenever $x^2 - 2x - 8 = 0$. Factoring, we have:

$$(x - 4)(x + 2) = 0$$

Thus, the expression is undefined when $x = 4$ and when $x = -2$.

6 **D** There are 58 7th graders who participate in 0–2 (i.e., fewer than 3 activities) out of 86 total 7th graders surveyed, giving a probability of $\frac{58}{86} = \frac{29}{43}$.

7 **D** Since 24% of juniors play a sport, 76% of juniors don't play a sport. Similarly, 80% of seniors don't play a sport.

76% of 150 is 114 juniors who don't play a sport, and 80% of 135 is 108 seniors who don't play a sport, so a total of 114 + 108 = 222 upperclassmen who don't play a sport, out of 285 total upperclassmen. 222 ÷ 285 ≈ 0.7789, approximately 78%.

8 B Here, we need to use the trigonometric identity $\sin a° = \cos (90 − a)°$, giving us $a = 90 − b$.

Since you're asked to find "a":

$$b = 90 − a$$

Thus, $a + 5 = 2(90 − a) − 13$

$$a + 5 = 180 − 2a − 13$$

Now, subtract 5 and add $2a$ on each side of the equation.

$$3a = 175 − 13$$
$$3a = 162$$
$$a = 54$$

9 B Since the circle has a diameter of $3x$, it has a circumference of $3x\pi$. Since the distance, travelling around the outside of the circle, from A to B is πx, in travelling from A to B, you've travelled $\frac{1}{3}$ of the way around the circle.

Thus, the measure of angle AOB is one-third of 2π, or $\frac{2\pi}{3}$

10 C 12 quizzes with an average score of 4.5 means that Pam has scored a total of $12(4.5) = 54$ points so far. Assuming she earns 5 points each on the next x quizzes, her total number of points will be $54 + 5x$, while the total number of quizzes taken will be $12 + x$. Thus, our equation is:

$$\frac{54 + 5x}{12 + x} = 4.6$$

$$54 + 5x = 4.6(12 + x)$$

$$54 + 5x = 55.2 + 4.6x$$

$$.4x = 1.2$$

$$x = 3$$

Note: you might work this problem more quickly by plugging in choices. Always plug in B or C first.

11 C Here, our denominator is the total number of students who didn't pass (61 + 89), and our numerator is the students who didn't pass but did attend the review session (61), giving us $\frac{61}{150}$

12 D Since Brian's Pizzeria is planning to buy 7 hours, Brian will qualify for the 20% discount. With a 20% discount applied, a 30-second commercial will cost $18.50(0.8) = $14.80.

The total number of 30-second commercials that can fit into 7 hours is 7 × 60 (minutes per hour) × 2 (30 second commercials per minute), which is 7(60)(2) = 840.

Buying 840 commercials at $14.80 each, Brian will spend $12,432.

13 B To increase a number by 2.5%, multiply it by 1.025 (thus, we can eliminate A and C). Because this growth only happens once every six years (as opposed to 6 times per year), we divide the exponent by 6, giving us choice B.

14 A Two and a half hours is 2.5(60) = 150 minutes. Thus we have:

$$\frac{3}{5} = \frac{x}{150}$$

$$450 = 5x$$

$$x = 90$$

15 A We can eliminate C and D right away, because the table tells us nothing about overall budget.

If we look at the Northeast, we can see that it took, on average, $11.51 in online advertising dollars to generate a shoe purchase, whereas it only took $8.15 in TV advertising dollars to generate a shoe purchase. This tells that TV advertising was more effective in the Northeast than online advertising, leading us to choice A.

16 C Again, it's critical to understand what the numbers mean—in this case, how much an advertiser has to spend in order to get one person to buy the shoes. "More effective" advertising means you're spending less money on average per person that you convince to buy the product. In the West, the advertiser has to spend $14.06 on TV ads in order to get one person to buy the shoes, but only $12.90 on online ads to accomplish the same thing, meaning that in the West, online ads are more effective than TV ads.

17 D The original equation factors as $y = (x - 4)(x + 7)$. An equation with the same x-intercepts but a different vertex can be obtained by reflecting the first parabola in the x-axis:

$$-(x - 4)(x + 7) = (4 - x)(x + 7)$$

18   12

Remember to start on the inside and work your way out. $g(7) = 4$.

From there, $f(4) = 12$.

19   119

Between 12:30 and 3:15, there are 2 hours and 45 minutes, or 2.75 hours.

2.75 hours is 2.75(60) = 165 minutes, so she will sell 165 ÷ 3 = 55 bottles between 12:30 and 3:15. Added to the 40 already sold, the vendor is at 95 bottles for the day. $95 \times 1.25 = \$118.75$

20   1572

8 years will pass between January 1, 2003 and December 31, 2010, so the population on December 31, 2010 was (according to the model) $170{,}000(1.003)^8$. Similarly, the population on December 31, 2013 was $170{,}000(1.003)^{11}$. Thus, the difference is $170{,}000(1.003)^{11} - 170{,}000(1.003)^8 = 1571.814$, which, rounded to the nearest whole number, is 1572.

Math Workout C: Calculator Permitted Item Breakout

ITEM	KEY	SKILL	CONTENT DIMENSION
1	C	Additional Topics in Math	Use concepts and theorems about congruence and similarity to solve problems about lines, angles, and triangles
2	A	Problem Solving and Data Analysis	Given a scatterplot, use linear, quadratic, or exponential models to describe how the variables are related
3	B	Problem Solving and Data Analysis	Use ratios, rates, proportional relationships, and scale drawings to solve single- and multi-step problems
4	A	Problem Solving and Data Analysis	Solve single- and multi-step problems involving percentages
5	C	Passport to Advanced Math	Rewrite simple rational expressions
6	D	Problem Solving and Data Analysis	Use two-way tables to summarize categorical data and relative frequencies, and calculate conditional probability
7	D	Problem Solving and Data Analysis	Solve single- and multi-step problems involving percentages
8	B	Additional Topics in Math	Use the relationship between similarity, right triangles, and trigonometric ratios; use the relationship between sine and cosine of complementary angles
9	B	Additional Topics in Math	Convert between degrees and radians and use radians to determine arc lengths; use trigonometric functions of radian measure
10	C	Heart of Algebra	Solve linear equations
11	C	Problem Solving and Data Analysis	Use two-way tables to summarize categorical data and relative frequencies, and calculate conditional probability
12	D	Problem Solving and Data Analysis	Solve single- and multi-step problems involving measurement quantities, units, and unit conversion
13	B	Passport to Advanced Math	Create a quadratic or exponential function
14	A	Heart of Algebra	Create, solve, or interpret linear equations in one variable
15	A	Problem Solving and Data Analysis	Use two-way tables to summarize categorical data and relative frequencies, and calculate conditional probability
16	C	Problem Solving and Data Analysis	Use two-way tables to summarize categorical data and relative frequencies, and calculate conditional probability
17	D	Passport to Advanced Math	Understand the relationship between zeros and factors of polynomials; use it to sketch graphs
18	12	Passport to Advanced Math	Use function notation, and interpret statements using function notation
19	119	Problem Solving and Data Analysis	Solve single- and multi-step problems involving measurement quantities, units, and unit conversion
20	1572	Heart of Algebra	Interpret the variables and constants in expressions for linear functions within the context presented

Math Workout D: No Calculator

1 **A** $(x + 3)(7 - 2) = 20$
$$(x + 3)5 = 20$$
$$5x + 15 = 20$$
$$5x = 5$$
$$x = 1$$

2 **D** The table tells us that $f(x) = 0$ when $x = -1$ and when $x = 2$. Since $-1 + 1 = 0$ and $2 - 2 = 0$, we derive the equation $(x + 1)(x - 2) = 0$.

3 **B** The sum of angles of a triangle is 180°. In this triangle, one of the angles measures 32°, and the other two are divided into four equal parts. Subtract 32° from 180° to get the total of the four equal parts. Divide this sum by four to get the value of n.

$$180° - 32° = 148°$$
$$\frac{148°}{4} = 37°$$
$$n = 37$$

4 **D** Distributing the negative, Y becomes $a^2 - c^2$. After multiplying X by $\frac{3}{4}$, we get $-3a^2 - 9c^2 + 12$. Thus, we need to evaluate the following:

$$a^2 - c^2 - (-3a^2 - 9c^2 + 12) = a^2 - c^2 + 3a^2 + 9c^2 - 12$$
$$= 4a^2 + 8c^2 - 12$$

5 **A** The term $.75ps$ indicates that it takes .75 minutes to grade a problem. This must be multiplied by s, the total number of students, since each student will have work for each problem. .75 minutes is 45 seconds.

6 **C** If the system has infinitely many solutions, then the line represented by the top equation must be the same as the line represented by the bottom equation. Since the lines are the same, the slope (or the opposite of the ratio of the coefficient of x and the coefficient of y) must be the same as well. So the slope: $-\frac{7}{5} = -\frac{a}{b}$, and $\frac{a}{b} = \frac{7}{5}$.

7 **C** $\frac{x + 20}{x + 2} = -\frac{8}{1}$

Cross multiplying we get
$$x + 20 = -8x - 16$$
$$9x + 20 = -16$$
$$9x = -36$$
$$x = -4$$

8 B We need $\dfrac{x^{2^a}}{x^{4^b}} > 1$

For this, we need the numerator to be greater than the denominator. Thus, we need $2^a > 4^b$. Note: This only holds if $x > 1$.

Since $4 = 2^2$, we can rewrite this as
$2^a > (2^2)^b$

Using laws of exponents, we get
$2^a > 2^{2b}$

So we need $a > 2b$

9   3

The two $5 gift cards and two $20 gift cards bring us to $50, so there are $35 left. Two additional $20 gift cards would take us over that limit, meaning that there is at most one additional $20 gift card, making the maximum 3. If you said 1, make sure to re-read and think about the initial two $20 gift cards.

10   6

Factoring a 6 out of the original expression, we get $6(x^2 - 9)$. The key here is to recognize $x^2 - 9$ as the difference of perfect squares, re-writing it as $6(x + 3)(x - 3)$. Thus, the sum we need is $6 + 3 + (-3) = 6$.

Math Workout D: No Calculator Item Breakout

ITEM	KEY	SKILL	CONTENT DIMENSION
1	A	Heart of Algebra	Create, solve, or interpret linear equations in one variable
2	D	Passport to Advanced Math	Understand the relationship between zeros and factors of polynomials; use it to sketch graphs
3	B	Additional Topics	Use concepts and theorems about congruence and similarity to solve problems about lines, angles, and triangles
4	D	Passport to Advanced Math	Add, subtract, and mulitiply polynomial expressions
5	A	Heart of Algebra	Interpret the variables and constants in expressions for linear functions within the context presented
6	C	Heart of Algebra	Understand connections between algebraic and graphical representations
7	C	Heart of Algebra	Create, solve, or interpret linear equations in one variable
8	B	Passport to Advanced Math	Solve an equation in one variable that contains radicals or contains the variable in the denominator of a fraction
9	3	Heart of Algebra	Create, solve, or interpret systems of two linear equations in two variables
10	6	Passport to Advanced Math	Solve a quadratic equation

Math Workout D: Calculator Permitted Answer Explanations

1   B   We're given the formula:

$$C = \frac{5}{9}(F - 32)$$

Using inverse operations, we get:

$$\frac{9}{5}C = F - 32$$

$$\frac{9}{5}C + 32 = F$$

Using this formula, Austin has a Fahrenheit temperature of 80.6, and Buffalo has a Fahrenheit temperature of 57.2, which is a difference of 23.4.

2   C   The mode, 15, will not be affected, so we can eliminate A immediately.

The current mean (average) is 18.9. With Anchorage included (and remembering to divide by 11 instead of 10) we get a new mean of $16.\overline{72}$.

The current median is 18. With Anchorage included, the median will still be 18.

3   C

$$102 - 8x = 42$$
$$102 = 42 + 8x$$
$$60 = 8x$$
$$7.5 = x$$
$$6(7.5) + 30 = 75$$

4   C   We can ZAP A and D because a squared (real) quantity cannot be negative. And B would have a radical solution. Thus C must be the correct answer. Alternatively you may complete the square:

$$x^2 - 14x + 45 = 0$$
$$x^2 - 14x = -45$$
$$x^2 - 14x + 49 = -45 + 49$$
$$x^2 - 14x + 49 = 4$$
$$(x - 7)^2 = 4$$

Note: You may prefer to solve for x in the original equation:

$$x^2 - 14x + 45 = 0$$
$$(x - 9)(x - 5) = 0$$
$$\{9, 5\}$$

Next, substitute 9 and 5 into the choices.

5   A   To answer this question, simply ask yourself: At what point will the first tank have been filling up 3 times as long as the second tank? Try out the times in the choices.

TIME	TANK 1 – time filling	TANK 2 – time filling	RATIO
1:30	1.5	.5	3:1
2:00	2	1	2:1
2:30	2.5	1.5	5:3
3:00	3	2	3:2
3:30	3.5	2.5	7:5

At 1:30 the first tank will have been filling $1\frac{1}{2}$ hours and the second tank $\frac{1}{2}$ hour.

$3 \times \frac{1}{2} = 1\frac{1}{2}$. You have your answer.

6   A   The solid line has the equation
$y = 7 - x$ OR $y = -x + 7$

In standard form, this is
$x + y = 7$
Allowing us to eliminate choices B and D.

Because the line is solid, the inequality is $\leq$ as opposed to $<$, giving us answer choice A.

7   A   <u>Statement I</u>: Average (Arithmetic Mean)

Average = Total ÷ Number

$60 + 65 + 70 + 85 + 90 + 90 + 100 = 560$
$$A = 560 \div 7 = 80$$

The average is NOT greater than 85, therefore Statement I is FALSE. *ZAP* B and D.

<u>Statement II</u>: Median (the middle number in an ordered list). In this case, the middle number is 85. Since 85 is NOT greater than 85, Statement II is FALSE. *ZAP* C.

<u>Statement III</u>: Mode (number occuring most frequently). The only number repeated in this list is 90, which is greater than 85. Statement III is TRUE. Choice A is corrrect.

8   D   As a decimal, .4% is 0.004. Adding this to 1 to show growth by .4%, we get 1.004, leading to our final expression, $1,200,000(1.004)^y$

9 **A** For each pool, there is a dot on the graph that shows its temperature in June along the horizontal axis and its temperature in July along the vertical axis. To figure out which pool had the greatest difference in temperature from June to July, find each pool's temperature from June and July, and then find the difference between the two.

Pool	June Temp.	July Temp.	Difference
1	72	77	+5
2	72	74	+2
3	74	75	+1
4	74	74	+0
5	75	72	−3

10 **B** The median of a set of numbers is the middle number in the set. If there is an even number of numbers in the set, the median is the average of the middle two numbers. In this problem, there are ten numbers. The median is the average of the fifth and sixth numbers. Both of these numbers are 74. Therefore, the median is also 74.

11 **B** $7x - 16 \geq 9x - 2$
$-2x - 16 \geq -2$
$-2x \geq 14$

Remembering to flip the inequality sign when dividing by a negative coefficient: $x \leq -7$

The greatest integer that's less than or equal to −7 is −7.

12 **D** Choice A shows a positive association. Choices B and C show little or no association at all. The line of best fit for choice D, however, is clearly sloping downward, making it the correct answer.

13 **B** There is more than one way to solve this problem. You can divide the given figure into two separate figures, find the areas of each of the new figures, then add the two areas together. 30 + 56 = 86 sq. ft.

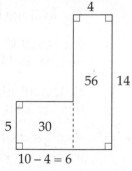

14 C A vertical line has no slope, or its slope is undefined. Line l must be vertical, as shown below:

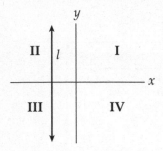

15 D $g(f(7)) = g(2) = 12$

16 D The mode of a set of numbers is the number that occurs most frequently. If Jackie drops her lowest score, 81, the mode will be 94 because it appears more than any number in the set.

17 B Remember, the following equation represents a circle with center (h, k) and radius r:
$(x - h)^2 + (y - k)^2 = r^2$

We essentially need to complete the square twice here. Half of -4 is -2, and $(-2)^2 = 4$. Half of 12 is 6, and $6^2 = 36$. From this, the left side of our equation becomes
$x^2 - 4x + 4 + y^2 + 12y + 36$

Adding $(4 + 36)$ to the right side, we get a new equation:
$x^2 - 4x + 4 + y^2 + 12y + 36 = 9$

Factoring, we get:
$(x - 2)^2 + (y + 6)^2 = 9$

Thus, the center of the circle is $(2, -6)$

18 $\frac{1}{3}$ or .333

You are given a in terms of b and ac in terms of b. Plug the value of a into $ac = \frac{5}{(18b)}$ and then solve for c.

$ac = \frac{5}{(18b)}$

$\frac{5}{(6b)} \bullet c = \frac{5}{(18b)}$

$c = \frac{5}{(18b)} \times \frac{(6b)}{5}$ (Remember, to divide by a fraction, multiply by its reciprocal.)

$c = \frac{6b}{18b}$

$c = \frac{1}{3}$

19   0

Solve the equation for p.

$$(p - 6)^2 = (p + 6)^2$$
$$(p - 6)(p - 6) = (p + 6)(p + 6) \quad \text{Expand each side.}$$
$$p^2 - 12p + 36 = p^2 + 12p + 36$$
$$-12p = 12p \qquad \text{Subtract } p^2 \text{ and 36.}$$
$$-p = p \qquad \text{Divide by 12.}$$

The only value where $-p = p$ is 0.

20   252

Since sine is opposite/hypotenuse, we can set up a diagram of a similar triangle as follows:

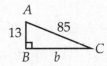

Using the Pythagorean Theorem, we get
$13^2 + b^2 = 85^2$

Solving, we get $b = 84$.

From there, knowing that $AB = 39$ (as opposed to 13), we can use the following proportion:

$\frac{13}{39} = \frac{84}{b}$

Solving, we get $b = 252$

Math Workout D: Calculator Permitted Item Breakout

ITEM	KEY	SKILL	CONTENT DIMENSION
1	B	Heart of Algebra	Build a linear function that models a linear relationship between two quantities
2	C	Problem Solving and Data Analysis	Use statistics to investigate measures of center of data and analyze shape, center, and spread
3	C	Heart of Algebra	Solve linear equations in one variable
4	C	Passport to Advanced Math	Create an equivalent form of an algebraic expression
5	A	Heart of Algebra	Create, solve, or interpret a linear equation in one variable
6	A	Heart of Algebra	Create, solve, or interpret systems of linear inequalities in two variables
7	A	Problem Solving and Data Analysis	Use statistics to investigate measures of center of data and analyze shape, center, and spread
8	D	Passport to Advanced Math	Create a quadratic or exponential function
9	A	Problem Solving and Data Analysis	Use the relationship between two variables to investigate key features of the graph
10	B	Problem Solving and Data Analysis	Use statistics to investigate measures of center of data and analyze shape, center, and spread
11	B	Heart of Algebra	Create, solve, or interpret linear inequalities in one variable
12	D	Problem Solving and Data Analysis	Given a scatterplot, use linear, quadratic, or exponential models to describe how the variables are related
13	B	Heart of Algebra	Create, solve, or interpret linear equations in one variable
14	C	Heart of Algebra	Understand connections between algebraic and graphical representations
15	D	Passport to Advanced Math	Use function notation, and interpret statements using function notation
16	D	Problem Solving and Data Analysis	Use statistics to investigate measures of center of data and analyze shape, center, and spread
17	B	Additional Topics in Math	Create or use an equation in two variables to solve a problem about a circle in the coordinate plane
18	$\frac{1}{3}$ or .333	Passport to Advanced Math	Use structure to isolate or identify a quantity of interest
19	0	Passport to Advanced Math	Solve a quadratic equation
20	252	Additional Topics in Math	Use trigonometric ratios and the Pythagorean Theorem

Math Workout E: No Calculator

1 D There are 215 students using 150 lockers. Label the number of lockers used by one student as $1x$. The number of lockers used by two students must be $2(150-x)$ because this is the total number of lockers minus the number of lockers that are used by only one student.

215 (students) − 150 (lockers) = 65 (students who must share a locker)   OR

150 − 65 = 85 (lockers used by only one student)

$$(1)x + 2(150 - x) = 215$$
$$x + 300 - 2x = 215$$
$$x - 2x = 215 - 300$$
$$-x = -85$$
$$x = 85$$

2 A If you multiply any number of perfect squares together, you will get another perfect square. Using this rule, you can *ZAP* all of the choices except A. If you want to double-check, find the square root of each choice. Only A does not have an integer square root.

3 C Sketching the graph, we see that the line passes through quadrants I, II, and IV, but not III.

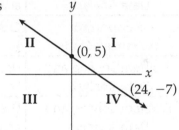

4 B Completing the square (take half of 14, square it, and add to both sides), we get:
$c^2 - 14c + 49 = 3$

Factoring, we get:
$(c - 7)^2 = 3$

Taking the square roots of both sides, we get two equations:
$c - 7 = \sqrt{3}$
and
$c - 7 = -\sqrt{3}$

This gives us two solutions:
$c = \sqrt{3} + 7$
$c = -\sqrt{3} + 7$
The greater of which is $\sqrt{3} + 7$

You may prefer to use the Quadratic Formula.

5 **A** Recall that $x^{\frac{3}{2}} = \sqrt{x^3}$

Since $7 = \sqrt{49}$, $7x^{\frac{3}{2}} = \sqrt{49} \cdot \sqrt{x^3}$

So $\sqrt{49x^3} = \sqrt{392}$

$\qquad 49x^3 = 392$

$\qquad\quad x^3 = 8$

$\qquad\quad\ x = 2$

6 **B** Since every two adjacent sections multiply together to make 18, start with the six and work up to x on both sides.

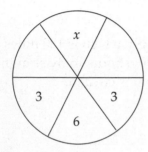 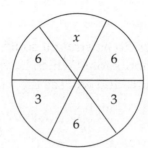 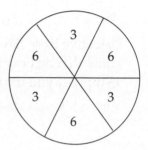

The value of x has to be 3.

7 **C** Solve the first equation for y.

$3y + 3y + 3y = 18$

$\qquad\qquad 9y = 18$

$\qquad\qquad\ y = \dfrac{18}{9}$

$\qquad\qquad\ y = 2$

Substitute the value of y into the second equation.

$\quad 3y - 1 =$

$(3 \times 2) - 1 =$

$\quad\ 6 - 1 = 5$

8 **A** In general, $x^{\frac{a}{b}} = \sqrt[b]{x^a}$. In this case, $w^{\frac{5}{4}} = \sqrt[4]{w^5}$

9   .60 or .6

If 36 cookies were purchased, it would take 6 boxes of 6 cookies at $3.60 each, or 3 boxes of 12 cookies at $7.00 each.

$3.60   or $7.00
×   6   ×   3
$21.60 $21.00

Find the difference between the two costs.
$21.60 − 21.00 = .60$

Note: Disregard the dollar sign when you grid-in your answer.

10   150

Detective Ross flew for three hours straight south at 40 mph, which is 120 miles. You also know that he flew for five hours total, which leaves him two hours to fly straight west at 45 mph. If you draw a picture, you will see the triangle that is created.

Detective Ross's Ranch

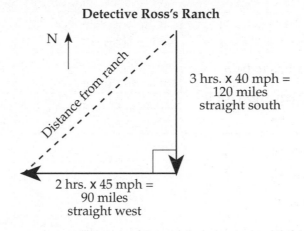

Now use the Pythagorean theorem   OR
to find the third side of the triangle,
and the answer to the problem.

$$a^2 + b^2 = c^2$$
$$120^2 + 90^2 = c^2$$
$$14400 + 8100 = c^2$$
$$22500 = c^2$$
$$c = 150$$

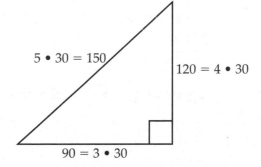

This is a 3-4-5 right triangle, scaled by a factor of 30.

Math Workout E: No Calculator Item Breakout

ITEM	KEY	SKILL	CONTENT DIMENSION
1	D	Heart of Algebra	Create, solve, or interpret systems of two linear equations in two variables
2	D	Passport to Advanced Math	Determine the most suitable form of an expression
3	C	Heart of Algebra	Understand connections between algebraic and graphical representations
4	B	Passport to Advanced Math	Solve a quadratic equation
5	A	Passport to Advanced Math	Determine the most suitable form of an expression
6	B	Passport to Advanced Math	Solve single- and multi-step problems involving measurement quantities, units, and unit conversion
7	C	Heart of Algebra	Create, solve, or interpret linear equations in one variable
8	A	Passport to Advanced Math	Create equivalent expressions involving rational exponents and radicals
9	.60 or .6	Problem Solving and Data Analysis	Solve single- and multi-step problems involving measurement quantities, units, and unit conversions.
10	150	Additional Topics	Use trigonometric ratios and the Pythagorean Theorem to solve applied problems involving right triangles

Math Workout E: Calculator Permitted Answer Explanations

1 D We know that 20 students were surveyed out of 140, and that Kelsey's ultimate margin of victory is 21 votes. Thus, we have:

$$\frac{x}{20} = \frac{21}{140}$$

Where x represents Kelsey's lead in the 20-student sample. Solving this proportion gives $x = 3$, so we need an answer choice where Kelsey wins and beats the second place finisher by 3 votes.

2 C $P = \dfrac{A}{1 + rt}$

$P(1 + rt) = A$

$1 + rt = \dfrac{A}{P}$

$rt = \dfrac{A}{P} - 1$

$t = \dfrac{\dfrac{A}{P} - 1}{r}$

3 C You can work this problem in two ways. One is a quick process of elimination. You know that $m + n = 10$ and $mn = 16$, so both variables must be positive numbers less than 10. Start by plugging in combinations: $9 + 1 = 10$, but $9 \times 1 = 9$. Doesn't work. $8 + 2 = 10$ and $8 \times 2 = 16$. You've got the values for m and n, so subtract them: $8 - 2 = 6$.

The other way to solve this problem is to solve one of the variables in terms of the other.

$$
\begin{aligned}
m + n &= 10 \\
m &= 10 - n \\
mn &= 16 \\
n(10 - n) &= 16 \\
10n - n^2 - 16 &= 0 && \text{Set all terms equal to zero.} \\
n^2 - 10n + 16 &= 0 && \text{Multiply both sides by } {}^-1. \\
(n - 8)(n - 2) &= 0 && \text{Factor.} \\
n - 8 = 0 \ \ &or \ \ n - 2 = 0 && \text{Set each factor equal to zero.} \\
n = 8 \quad & \quad \ n = 2
\end{aligned}
$$

If n can be either 8 or 2, then so can m. You can see from the choices that your answer must be positive, so m must be greater than n.

$m = 8$
$n = 2$
$m - n = 6$

4 **B** Use the area of a rectangle and area of a triangle formulas for this problem. The area of the entire square is $4 \times 4 = 16$. You know that segments UW and VY are 2 units because U and V are midpoints of ZW and ZY, respectively. Find the areas of triangles UWX and VYX and subtract these from the area of the entire square. This will give you the area of the quadrilateral $ZUXV$. Since UWX and VYX are right triangles, you know you can use their short sides as the height (H) in the following formulas.

Step 1: Find the area of triangle UWX.

$$A = \frac{1}{2}B \times H$$

$$A = \frac{1}{2}WX \times UW$$

$$A = \frac{1}{2}(4 \times 2) \quad A \text{ of triangle } UWX = 4$$

Step 2: Because triangle VYX has the same dimensions as triangle UWX, it also has an area of 4. The area of both triangles together $= 4 + 4 = 8$.

Step 3: Subtract the combined area of the two triangles from the area of the square. $16 - 8 = 8$ The area of quadrilateral $ZUXV$ is 8.

5 **B**

$$\frac{h}{g} = \frac{3h + g}{7}$$

$$\frac{h}{7} = \frac{3h + 7}{7} \qquad \text{Substitute 7 for } g.$$

$$\frac{(7)h}{7} = \frac{3h + 7}{7}(7) \qquad \text{Multiply both sides by 7 to eliminate the denominator.}$$

$$h = 3h + 7$$

$$-2h = 7$$

$$h = -\frac{7}{2}$$

$$h = -3.5$$

6 **A**

$$12 - \left| x - 3 \right| = 3$$

$$-\left| x - 3 \right| = -9$$

$$\left| x - 3 \right| = 9$$

$$x - 3 = 9$$

$$x = 12$$

OR

$$x - 3 = -9$$

$$x = -6$$

7 A Let x = number of hot dogs and y number of hamburgers sold. We need to solve the following system of equations:

$2.5x + 3.5y = 243$
$x + y = 80$

Multiplying the bottom equation by 2.5, we get:

$2.5x + 3.5y = 243$
$2.5x + 2.5y = 200$

Subtracting the bottom equation from the top one, we get:

$y = 43$

Thus, there were 43 hamburgers sold and 37 hot dogs sold. The 37 hot dogs brought in a total of $37(2.5) = \$92.5$ in revenue. $\frac{92.5}{243}$ is approximately .3806, or 38%.

8 A This question first asks, "To what power, x, must you raise 3 in order to get 27?" In other words, how many times must you multiply 3 times itself in order to get 27?

$3 \times 3 \times 3 = 27$
So, $x = 3$.

The second part of the question asks you to find the value of 4 to the $x - 1$ power. You know that $x = 3$, so $x - 1 = 2$. Now you have 4^2, which is $4 \times 4 = 16$.

9 B To calculate the percent change, we divide the change by the original (2014–2015) amount. This gives us 6.7% for athletics, 9.8% for drama, and 3.3% for music.

10 D The total 2015–2016 budget was 200,000. 96% of this is $.96(200,000) = 192,000$ for 2016–2017.

The 2016–2017 athletics budget will be $.98(80,000) = 78,400$

The 2016–2017 music budget will be $.99(63,000) = 62,370$

We're given that the uncategorized budget will be 10,000.

Subtracting these figures from 192,000, we're left with $41,230 for drama.

11 C To simplify, we need to multiply both the numerator and denominator by the conjugate of the denominator:

$$\frac{7 - 3i}{12 + i} \times \frac{12 - i}{12 - i}$$

$$\frac{84 - 43i + 3i^2}{144 - i^2}$$

$$\frac{84 - 43i - 3}{144 + 1}$$

$$\frac{81 - 43i}{145}$$

$$\frac{81}{145} - \frac{43i}{145}$$

12　A　In factored form, the equation could be:
$$x(x + 2)(x - 5)$$
$$x(x^2 - 3x - 10)$$
$$x^3 - 3x^2 - 10x$$

13　C　Setting the denominator equal to 0, we get $x^2 - 2x - 8 = 0$

Factoring, we obtain:
$$(x - 4)(x + 2) = 0$$

Setting each factor equal to 0, we get two undefined values:
$x - 4 = 0$ give us $x = 4$
$x + 2 = 0$ gives us $x = -2$

14　A　2.5 hours is 150 minutes. There will be $\frac{150}{5} = 30$ five-minute periods within 2.5 hours.

15　B　As x increases, $f(x)$ decreases, meaning that we have a negative slope and can eliminate choices A and C.

Using the first two points we're given $(-2, 7)$ and $(-1, 4)$, we can calculate a slope of -3, leading to answer choice B.

Or, another way is to substitute ordered pairs from the table (start with ordered pair $(0,1)$).

16　D　This is a "triple true/false" problem. The sum of a and b is negative. Using this information, plug in a few numbers and see which statements could be true.

<u>Statement I</u>. $-2 < -1 < 0$ and $-2 + -1 = -3$, so this could be true. *ZAP* choices B and C.

<u>Statement II</u>. Since you've ZAPPED B and C, there's no need to test Statement II.

<u>Statement III</u>. $-2 < 0 < 1$ and $-2 + 1 = -1$, so this could be true.

Both Statements I and III could be true, so the answer is D.

17　D　The average amount each person would contribute before losing q people would be $\frac{M}{20}$.

If q people leave the group, the average contribution would be $\frac{M}{20 - q}$.

You could then use the equation $\frac{M}{20 - q} - \frac{M}{20} =$ Amount of increase per person.

Finding one term, do this:

$$\frac{20M}{(20 - q)20} - \frac{M(20 - q)}{(20 - q)20}$$

Simplifying: $\frac{Mq}{400 - 20q}$

18   $\frac{7}{13}$ or .538

The probability that a blue gumball will be drawn on the first draw is 8 out of 14 because there are 8 blue gumballs and 14 total. Once a blue gumball is drawn out of the jar, there are only 7 blue gumballs left and 13 total. The probability of drawing a blue one is now 7 out of 13, or $\frac{7}{13}$. This can also be converted into the decimal .538, but it is not necessary.

19   $\frac{8}{6}$ or $\frac{4}{3}$ or 1.33

The maximum possible value can only be found if g is the largest number in the set and h is the smallest.

$2\left(\frac{5}{6}\right) - 2\left(\frac{1}{6}\right) =$ Plug in the largest value for g and the smallest for h.

$\frac{10}{6} - \frac{2}{6} = \frac{8}{6}$ Multiply and subtract the two values.

Note: This can be reduced to $\frac{4}{3}$ or converted to 1.33, but all three answers are acceptable, so there is no need to spend extra time reducing.

20   12

Using a calculator to graph the two equations, we find that the one point of intersection is $(-3, -7)$. Since there is only one point of intersection, it must be the vertex of the parabola. You may use the method for finding the vertex.

$h = -\frac{b}{2a} = -\frac{6}{2} = -3$

$k = (-3)^2 + 6(-3) + 2$
$\quad = 9 - 18 + 2$
$\quad = -7$

The point of intersection is $(-3, -7)$.

$3(-3) - 3(-7) = 12$

Math Workout E: Calculator Permitted Item Breakout

ITEM	KEY	SKILL	CONTENT DIMENSION
1	D	Problem Solving and Data Analysis	Make inferences about population parameters based on sample data
2	C	Passport to Advanced Math	Use structure to isolate or identify a quantity of interest
3	C	Passport to Advanced Math	Use structure to isolate or identify a quantity of interest
4	B	Additional Topics in Math	Use concepts and theorems about congruence and similarity to solve problems about lines, angles, and triangles
5	B	Heart of Algebra	Create, solve, or interpret linear equations in one variable
6	A	Heart of Algebra	Create, solve, or interpret linear equations in one variable
7	A	Heart of Algebra	Create, solve, or interpret systems of two linear equations in two variables
8	A	Passport to Advanced Math	Create equivalent expressions involving radicals and rational exponents
9	B	Problem Solving and Data Analysis	Evaluate reports to make inferences, justify conclusions, and determine appropriateness of data collection methods
10	D	Problem Solving and Data Analysis	Evaluate reports to make inferences, justify conclusions, and determine appropriateness of data collection methods
11	C	Additional Topics in Math	Perform arithmetic operations on complex numbers
12	A	Passport to Advanced Math	Understand the relationship between zeros and factors of polynomials; use it to sketch graphs
13	C	Passport to Advanced Math	Solve an equation in one variable that contains radicals or contains the variable in the denominator of a fraction
14	A	Problem Solving and Data Analysis	Create quadratic or exponential functions
15	B	Heart of Algebra	Create, solve, or interpret a linear expression or equation in one variable
16	D	Heart of Algebra	Create, solve, or interpret systems of linear inequalities in two variables
17	D	Passport to Advanced Math	Rewrite simple rational expressions
18	$\frac{7}{13}$ or .538	Problem Soving and Data Analysis	Use two-way tables to summarize categorical data and relative frequencies, and calculate conditional probability
19	$\frac{8}{6}$ or $\frac{4}{3}$ or 1.33	Heart of Algebra	Build a linear function that models a linear relationship between two quantities
20	12	Passport to Advanced Math	Solve a system of equations consisting of one linear and one quadratic equation in two variables

Math Workout F: No Calculator

1 D We're given:
$$2x + 5y = 36$$
$$y = 3x - 20$$

Substituting for y, we get:
$$2x + 5(3x - 20) = 36$$
$$2x + 15x - 100 = 36$$
$$17x - 100 = 36$$
$$17x = 136$$
$$x = 8$$
$$y = 3(8) - 20 = 4$$
$$\frac{x}{y} = \frac{8}{4} = 2$$

2 B Knowing that Monday's lunch was more expensive than Tuesday's lunch allows us to eliminate choices A and C.

Monday's lunch cost $2 more, and a 20% tip, applied to the $2 difference, is 2(.2) = .4.

2 (extra for the sandwich) + .4 (extra for the tip) gives us a difference of $2.40.

3 B $3a + 4 = 12 - a$ Solve for a.
$$4a = 8$$
$$a = 2$$

4 A We can use FOIL here:
$$(7 - 2i)(5 + i)$$
$$35 + 7i - 10i - 2i^2$$
$$35 - 3i - 2(-1)$$
$$37 - 3i$$

5 C $120^2 = r(60^2)$ Solve for r.

$r = \frac{120^2}{60^2}$ Divide both sides by 60^2.

$r = \frac{120 \times 120}{60 \times 60}$ Square.

$r = \frac{12 \times 12}{6 \times 6}$ Drop the zeros to simplify.

$r = 2 \times 2$ Simplify again.

$r = 4$

6 A The equation we need to solve is:

$$x^2 - 2x - 9 = 6$$
$$x^2 - 2x - 15 = 0$$
$$(x - 5)(x + 3) = 0$$
$$x = 5 \text{ or } x = -3$$

Since $d > c$, $d = 5$ and $c = -3$
$$d - c = 5 - (-3) = 8$$

7 D From the information given, we have:
$$h(x) = c(x + 4)(x - 7)$$

Since all the possible quadratics have a leading coefficient of 1, c must equal 1.

$$h(x) = (x + 4)(x - 7) \qquad \text{(Multiply the factors.)}$$
$$h(x) = x^2 - 3x - 28$$

8 C For two lines to be perpendicular, their slopes need to be opposite reciprocals, so the slope of the line in our answer needs to be $-\frac{5}{4}$.

Finding the slopes of the lines given, we see that answer choice C has a slope of $-\frac{5}{4}$.

9 64

We're given the equation
$$x^5 - 20x^3 = -64x$$
$$x^5 - 20x^3 + 64x = 0$$
$$x(x^4 - 20x^2 + 64) = 0$$
$$x(x^2 - 16)(x^2 - 4) = 0$$
$$x(x - 4)(x + 4)(x - 2)(x + 2) = 0$$

The four possible nonzero values of x are thus $4, -4, 2,$ and -2. Their product is
$$4(-4)(2)(-2) = 64$$

10 55

The larger integer is 23 greater than the smaller one.
$$x = \text{larger integer}$$
$$x - 23 = \text{smaller integer}$$
The sum of the two integers is 87.

$$x + x - 23 = 87$$
$$2x - 23 = 87$$
$$2x = 87 + 23$$
$$2x = 110$$
$$x = 55$$

Math Workout F: No Calculator Item Breakout

ITEM	KEY	SKILL	CONTENT DIMENSION
1	D	Heart of Algebra	Solve systems of two linear equations in two variables
2	B	Heart of Algebra	Build a linear function that models a linear relationship between two quantities
3	B	Heart of Algebra	Create, solve, or interpret linear equations in one variable
4	A	Additional Topics	Perform arithmetic operations on complex numbers
5	C	Passport to Advanced Math	Create, solve, or interpret linear equations in one variable
6	A	Passport to Advanced Math	Solve a quadratic equation
7	D	Passport to Advanced Math	Understand the relationship between zeros and factors of polynomials; use it to sketch graphs
8	C	Heart of Algebra	Understand connections between algebraic and graphical representations
9	64	Passport to Advanced Math	Understand the relationship between zeros and factors of polynomials; use it to sketch graphs
10	55	Heart of Algebra	Solve systems of two linear equations in two variables

Math Workout F: Calculator Permitted Answer Explanations

1   A   All you have to do here is simplify.

$$\frac{\left(\frac{1}{x} - y\right)x}{\left(x - \frac{1}{x}\right)x} = \frac{1 - xy}{x^2 - 1}$$

2   C   Our inequality is

$$\frac{2}{3}x - 7 > x - 18$$

$$-\frac{1}{3}x - 7 > -18$$

$$-\frac{1}{3}x > -11$$

$$x < 33$$

(Remember to flip the inequality sign when multiplying by -3.)

The greatest integer that's less than 33 is 32.

3   A   The average is found by adding the expressions together and then dividing by the number of expressions added together.

$$\frac{(7n + 1) + (n - 7)}{2} = \frac{8n - 6}{2} = \frac{2(4n - 3)}{2} = 4n - 3$$

4   C   To find the slope of a line, you divide the amount of (vertical) change in the y-variable by the amount of (horizontal) change in the x-variable. You can think of this as the rise over the run. Pick two points on the line and substitute their coordinates into the equation:

$$\text{slope} = \frac{y_2 - y_1}{x_2 - x_1}$$

Points (2,4) and (8,6) are easy to use.

$$\text{slope} = \frac{(6 - 4)}{(8 - 2)}$$

$$\text{slope} = \frac{2}{6} = \frac{1}{3}$$

Note: You can ZAP choices A and B because it's an upward slope, indicating that the answer must be positive.

5   D   Graphing the two equations ($y = x^2 + 7x - 5$ and $y = 3x + 7$), we can see that there are two intersections.

Alternatively, we can solve the equation $x^2 + 7x - 5 = 3x + 7$ and see that there are two solutions.

6   C   In order to be a solution to the system of inequalities, a point needs to be in the region that was shaded twice. Note: Choice A $(-1, 3)$, lies on the dashed line. Points on the dashed line are not in the solution set.

7 **A** We're given $4x - 6 = -3$

$4x = 3$

$x = \dfrac{3}{4}$

From this,

$12\left(\dfrac{3}{4}\right) - 2 = 9 - 2 = 7$

8 **C** Because $WXYZ$ is a rectangle, you know that all the angles in it are 90°. This means that you can use the Pythagorean theorem ($a^2 + b^2 = c^2$) to find the length of segment WX.

$WX^2 + 8^2 = 10^2$
$WX^2 + 64 = 100$
$\quad WX^2 = 36$
$\quad\ WX = 6$

Now use the area formula to find the area of rectangle $WXYZ$.

$A = l \times w$
$A = 8 \times 6$
$A = 48$

9 **D** Because it's a line and it passes through (0,0), the relationship must be directly proportional ($y = kx$). You may use either given point for x and y values, substituting those values in the equation $y = kx$.

If $a = 2$, we have a constant of proportionality (k) of 4.

If $a = -2$, we have a constant of proportionality (k) of -4.

10 **C** Seven more students in Gabby's sample like science fiction movies. Using a proportion, we have:

$\dfrac{7}{30} = \dfrac{x}{270}$
$30x = 1890$
$\quad x = 63$

11 **B** Our height is 8 meters, and our diameter is 1.25(8) = 10 meters. This gives us a radius of 5 meters, and a volume of $8(5^2)\pi = 200\pi$.

12 B We're given:

$$\frac{1}{\frac{1}{x-6}+\frac{1}{x+2}}$$

Finding a common denominator, we get:

$$\frac{1}{\frac{x+2}{(x-6)(x+2)}+\frac{x-6}{(x-6)(x+2)}}$$

$$\frac{1}{\frac{(x+2)+(x-6)}{(x-6)(x+2)}}$$

$$\frac{1}{\frac{2x-4}{x^2-4x-12}}$$

$$\frac{x^2-4x-12}{2x-4}$$

13 D We're asked to evaluate

$$\frac{9x-5}{3x+1}$$

Doing polynomial long division, we have:

$$\begin{array}{r} 3 \\ 3x+1\overline{)9x-5} \\ \underline{-(9x+3)} \\ -8 \end{array}$$

$$3-\frac{8}{3x+1}$$

OR

$$\frac{9x-5}{3x+1}=\frac{9x+3-8}{3x+1}$$

$$=\frac{9x+3}{3x+1}-\frac{8}{3x+1}$$

$$=3-\frac{8}{3x+1}$$

14 B $f(-6x)=2(-6x)-9$
$\qquad\qquad=-12x-9$

15 D Because there are 200 people from Fountain Hills that were surveyed, we need to know how many hours of physical activity the middle (i.e. 100th) person gets. If you lined up the adults from least active to most active, the 100th most active person (i.e. the median person) gets 2 hours of exercise.

16 A It makes a difference *when* you combine the populations. Calculate the percentages separately first. *Then* combine the populations. In the sample, 90 of 200 people (45%) in Fountain Hills meet the criteria, and 96 of 200 people (48%) in Glendale meet the criteria. (.45)80,000 = 36,000 citizens of Fountain Hills and (.48)(120,000) = 57,600 people in Glendale who meet the criteria. Our total is 93,600.

17 B Let x = number of miles driven.

$$1.75+.8x+3=11.15$$
$$4.75+.8x=11.15$$
$$.8x=6.4$$
$$x=8$$

18 $\frac{1}{35}$ or .028 or .029

There were a total of 7,000 spam emails. Of these, the program identified 200 as non-spam. This gives us a probability of $\frac{200}{7000} = \frac{1}{35}$

19 199

$$400(1.035)^{20} - 300(1.035)^{20} = 198.9788863$$

20 5

Set up an equation to solve for m by taking the sum of all the expressions in the set and dividing by the number of expressions in the set, which is 5. This is equal to the average, which you're told is 4.

$$\frac{m + (m - 3) + (m - 4) + (m - 10) + (2m - 11)}{5} = 4$$

$$\frac{6m - 28}{5} = 4$$

$$6m - 28 = 20$$

$$6m = 48$$

$$m = 8$$

The mode is the most frequent number, which in this case is 5.

$m - 3 = 8 - 3 = 5$
and
$2m - 11 = 16 - 11 = 5$

Math Workout F: Calculator Permitted Item Breakout

ITEM	KEY	SKILL	CONTENT DIMENSION
1	A	Passport to Advanced Math	Choose and produce equivalent forms of expressions to reveal and explain properties of a quantity
2	C	Heart of Algebra	Create, solve, or interpret linear inequalities in one variable
3	A	Heart of Algebra	Create, solve, or interpret a linear expression in one variable
4	C	Heart of Algebra	Use the relationship between two variables to investigate key features of the graph
5	D	Passport to Advanced Math	Solve a system of equations consisting of one linear and one quadratic equation in two variables
6	C	Heart of Algebra	Create, solve, or interpret systems of linear inequalities in two variables
7	A	Heart of Algebra	Solve linear equations in one variable
8	C	Additional Topics	Use trigonometric ratios and the Pythagorean Theorem to solve applied problems involving right triangles
9	D	Heart of Algebra	Understand connections between algebraic and graphical representations
10	C	Problem Soving and Data Analysis	Make inferences about population parameters based on sample data
11	B	Additional Topics	Solve problems using volume formulas
12	B	Passport to Advanced Math	Rewrite simple rational expressions
13	D	Passport to Advanced Math	Rewrite simple rational expressions
14	B	Passport to Advanced Math	Use function notation, and interpret statements using function notation
15	D	Problem Soving and Data Analysis	Use statistics to investigate measures of center of data
16	A	Problem Soving and Data Analysis	Make inferences about population parameters based on sample data
17	B	Heart of Algebra	Create, solve, or interpret linear equations in one variable
18	$\frac{1}{35}$ or .028 or .029	Problem Soving and Data Analysis	Use two-way tables to summarize categorical data and relative frequencies, and calculate conditional probability
19	199	Passport to Advanced Math	Create quadratic or exponential functions
20	5	Problem Soving and Data Analysis	Use statistics to investigate measures of center of data and analyze shape, center, and spread

Reading Workout A

1 B Correa is described as having "his hands full" (another way of saying he had a challenge) after his election. The passage states that "half of the population lived at or below the poverty level," and the constitution of Ecuador has "protected rights" for the indigenous people and nature." The passage goes on to talk about how Correa had a difficult choice: how to balance the needs of his country's economy with the constitutional protections for nature and indigenous people.

2 A Lines 18–24 outline Correa's challenge, which involves upholding the constitution's protections of both indigenous people and the environment while dealing with a serious poverty problem that oil sales could help ameliorate.

3 D The language of the Ecuadorian constitution clearly forbids extractive activities in areas where indigenous people live and describes the ways in which the government is required to avoid ethnocide, or the destruction of an indigenous group.

4 C The constitution's strong language commands the government to protect the Amazon from destruction. If you're not sure which choice to pick, plug each one in. The language of the constitution is telling the government it has to protect the environment and indigenous people. The constitution is issuing a *command*, not an *accusation* (A), *attack* (B), or *supplies* (D).

5 B Lines 74 and 75 say that critics accused Correa of "holding the rainforest for ransom," until he could get money from the international community to protect it. When he "let the captive go," he freed the *rainforest* for development.

6 A The first mention of *ethnocide* closely follows mention of the constitutional protections for "the way of life and the land of indigenous people." See lines 31–36.

7 B The constitution says that violating the rights of indigenous people to be free from drilling "shall constitute a crime of ethnocide." The author follows that quote by saying, in lines 33–36, that *in other words*, drilling could *destroy the indigenous people's way of life*: their land, livelihood, and culture.

8 D The first two paragraphs describe the delicate balance between the requirement to protect the environment and indigenous peoples, and the lure of economic development from Ecuador's oil reserves. This sets up the discussion in the remainder of the passage.

9 C In the last paragraph, the author says that 70 percent of the Ecuadoran people hope that the Trust Fund initiative might still work as it was supposed to. This indicates that a majority of Ecuadorans would prefer to see the environment protected rather than open Yasuní for oil exploration.

10 B Because Ecuador sells more oil to the United States than any other country by a large margin, it is highly dependent on that economic relationship. Maintaining good relations with its South American neighbor (A) is likely a priority, but that is not mentioned in the graph. *ZAP* it. C is a misreading of the graph. D is actually true, but it's not possible to get that information from this graph.

11 A As it's used here, *become* means *to make Adams look good*. It would not look good for him to strike out the negative remarks about the king. To say that something makes you *look good* is to say that it *flatters* you.

12 C Adams could have chosen to describe the way in which he persuaded Jefferson to write the Declaration of Independence, just as he described other aspects of the process. By using dialogue, he gives immediacy to his exchange with Jefferson, which helps Timothy Pickering (the original recipient of Adams' letter) and future readers feel privy to the conversation.

13 D Adams gives his reasons in lines 44–49. Jefferson did, indeed, receive more votes than Adams, but Adams says that's why they were *both* selected to write the draft. You can immediately ZAP C, because Adams was less critical of King George than his peers were. B is never mentioned in the passage; ZAP it. Adams was lavish in his praise of Jefferson's talents; D is the best answer.

14 B Although Jefferson rarely spoke in the Continental Congress, he had a reputation for being a learned man. Lines 17–21 say Jefferson "brought with him a reputation for literature, science, and a happy talent for composition." When "writings of his were handed about," it became clear that he was the right person to write the Declaration of Independence.

15 C Adams disagreed with Jefferson on some points, writing, "There were expressions which I would not have inserted, if I had drawn it up…" There is no evidence in the passage for any of the other three choices.

16 A The last two paragraphs discuss Adams' objections to some of Jefferson's rhetoric, especially the example cited in lines 57–59 calling King George a tyrant.

17 D In lines 55–57, Adams discusses his delight with the quality of Jefferson's work, and refers to *flights of oratory*. It should be pretty clear that A, *journeys*, is wrong, so ZAP it. One meaning of *flight* is a set of stairs or steps, but that's not the context here, so ZAP C. Of the remaining choices, D should jump out at you if you know what *oratory* means. A *flight of oratory* is a display of great verbal skill. But even if you don't know this, the idea of escaping doesn't make much sense in context, and you should be able to ZAP B.

18 D Adams says that Jefferson's draft contained "expressions which I would not have inserted, if I had drawn it up, particularly that which called the King tyrant." He goes on to explain that he believed the king was "deceived by his courtiers" and only cruel in his official capacity, and not personally. ZAP C because, even if true, a discussion of the reasons for writing the Declaration of Independence is not included in the passage.

19 C In the letter, Adams describes how it was decided that Jefferson would write the Declaration of Independence and the result of that decision. Although the passage does begin with a question, it would be hard to argue that the question goes unanswered (A). The passage offers only Adams' perspective on the writing of the Declaration of Independence, not multiple perspectives (B). Although Adams discusses his personal objections to some of Jefferson's rhetoric, he never questions the decision to have Jefferson write the Declaration (D).

Reading Workout A Item Breakout

ITEM	KEY	SKILL	CONTENT DIMENSION
1	B	Close reading	Information and ideas
2	A	Text evidence	Information and ideas
3	D	Text structure	Rhetoric
4	C	Words in context	Information and ideas
5	B	Word choice	Rhetoric
6	A	Close reading	Information and ideas
7	B	Text evidence	Information and ideas
8	D	Text structure	Rhetoric
9	C	Close reading	Information and ideas
10	B	Quantitative information	Synthesis
11	A	Words in context	Information and ideas
12	C	Word choice	Rhetoric
13	D	Close reading	Information and ideas
14	B	Text evidence	Information and ideas
15	C	Central idea	Information and ideas
16	A	Text evidence	Information and ideas
17	D	Words in context	Rhetoric
18	D	Analyze argument	Rhetoric
19	C	Text structure	Rhetoric

Reading Workout B

1 D The passage describes several instances (not just one) that led to Paul's suspension from school. It also discusses the way he acts while asking to be reinstated. The author uses these incidents to flesh out his description of Paul as "hysterically defiant," contemptuous, and insolent.

2 D In line 13, *significant* is used as an adjective, although in an uncommon way. The best way to answer this question is to try each choice in place of *significant* and see which one makes the most sense. In context, *suggestive* is the best fit. The bright red carnation doesn't suggest (or *signify*) that Paul has the contrite spirit of someone who is truly sorry for his actions.

3 C The passage describes how Paul pulled away with a shudder when a teacher touched his hand. The choice that best describes this sudden movement is *jerked*.

4 A Although he is *polite* during the meeting with his principal and teachers and is well acquainted with *lying* (D), those are not the main behaviors he evidenced in his classes. Paul showed *disrespect* to his teachers by mocking them with a running commentary (lines 54–55). His showing *disrespect* in class contradicts his false *politeness* (D) in the meeting. Also see explanation for number 5, below.

5 C Paul has been suspended from school for various acts against his teachers. Lines 51–55 describe specific incidents of shading his eyes and looking out the window (signs of disinterest) or joking about the lecture (disrespect).

6 A Paul's teachers are clearly upset with his behavior in their classrooms and give several unflattering descriptions of his actions. You can quickly ZAP B, because Paul didn't strike his teacher; he put his hands behind him. See answer explanation for number 7 for further discussion.

7 C When Paul's teachers are asked to state their charges, they do so with "rancor and aggrievedness" (line 31), which indicates very strong feelings of anger. In lines 58 and 59, the author says the teachers "fell upon him without mercy." It's clear that Paul is being set upon harshly by his teachers, and "baptism of fire" is an effective metaphor for that treatment.

8 B There's nothing in the passage to indicate that the narrator is someone who has been victimized by Paul in the past (A) or is a student (D). An advocate pleading with the reader to understand Paul (C) would take a different tone. The tone of this passage is neutral and dispassionate. The narrator does not take a position on Paul, choosing instead to let the details of the story show what kind of person Paul is.

9 A At the end of the story, Paul has just endured a long series of complaints about his behavior from a group of teachers who obviously dislike him, yet he smiles and bows when he is dismissed. This is very much like responding to boos and catcalls, which are expressions of dislike, by waving in greeting. In both cases, the person who is the object of dislike appears not to be bothered by it, but to actually enjoy it.

10   D   *Nanotechnology* is described in Passage 1 as being about manipulating atoms and molecules. Later, the passage talks about making paper-thin speakers. There's no mention of making steel stronger (A), but of nanotubes being "stronger than steel." Presumably, traveling on a 62,000 mile elevator to space would not necessarily be faster than traveling in a rocket; regardless, there's no mention in the passage of the speed of travel (C). While there is mention of the possibility of carbon nanotubes causing lung disease, it's assumed this would be "similar" to current lung diseases from small particulates such as soot and asbestos; there's no hint that nanotubes would cause *new diseases* (B).

11   C   Passage 1 discusses uses for carbon nanotube semiconductors in lines 30 through 33. Roll-up smartphone screens, embedded windshield displays in cars, and paper-thin speakers are all examples of hardware that could be made much thinner than they are now with carbon nanotube technology.

12   B   The statement that countries have increased spending over the last decade is generally correct, although not all have done so at the same rate, and there was an occasional dip in spending (as a percentage of GDP) by some countries within this period. When referring specifically to the period between 2010 and 2012, all of the countries except Finland (from 3.88 to 3.55) and the United States (NA) show an increase. The United States is not listed as one of the choices, so Finland is correct.

13   A   In the context of cancer treatment, "no more operations!" most nearly means, "no more *surgical procedures*."

14   A   The author's lengthy explanation of the history of asbestos, including its widespread usage, its problems, and its continued use despite government attempts to regulate it, is presented as a cautionary tale for the use of carbon nanotubes—not for *warning against technological innovation* (B) in general. The physical resemblance of nanotubes to silica dust and the likelihood that they will be used in many, many everyday applications is reason for the author to express concern about them. Though government regulation of asbestos is mentioned, the author complains that it "falls far short of ensuring complete public safety," rather than *arguing in favor of government regulation* (C). The author of Passage 1 never compares *concerns* about asbestos and nanotube technology (D).

15   B   The author of Passage 2 writes, "But the useful properties of asbestos—and the profitability of asbestos-based products—kept many of these medical reports from reaching the public eye." It's reasonable to conclude that negative medical reports about asbestos-based products might have made them less popular and less profitable to produce. Therefore, companies making asbestos-based products would have a business interest in keeping these reports from becoming public.

16   B   Lines 64 through 67 directly connect "the useful properties of asbestos" and "the profitability of asbestos-based products" with the fact that "many of these medical reports" didn't get released to the public.

17 B   Passage 1 lists several ways in which carbon nanotubes might lead to technological advances. Passage 2 acknowledges the promise of carbon nanotubes but uses the example of asbestos to warn against possible dangers.

18 D   The author of Passage 1 acknowledges possible negatives regarding carbon nanotube technology in lines 45 and 46, so A can't be correct. B is untrue; scientists often develop technologies that are intended to be dangerous. There is no evidence in either passage for C. D is correct because the author of Passage 1 is extremely optimistic about the future, and he suggests in lines 45–47 that potential dangers can be overcome (even though he doesn't say precisely how).

19 C   The author of Passage 1 includes a great deal of evidence for his claim that carbon nanotube semiconductors will lead to great technological change. The author of Passage 2 acknowledges this in lines 75–78 by mentioning the promise of improvements to everyday products and the introduction of new ones previously unimagined.

Reading Workout B Item Breakout

ITEM	KEY	SKILL	CONTENT DIMENSION
1	D	Analyzing purpose	Rhetoric
2	D	Words in context	Information and ideas
3	C	Words in context	Information and ideas
4	A	Close reading	Information and ideas
5	C	Text evidence	Information and ideas
6	A	Understanding relationships	Information and ideas
7	C	Text evidence	Information and ideas
8	B	Point of view	Rhetoric
9	A	Close reading	Information and ideas
10	D	Close reading	Information and ideas
11	C	Text evidence	Information and ideas
12	B	Quantitative information	Synthesis
13	A	Words in context	Information and ideas
14	A	Text structure	Rhetoric
15	B	Understanding relationships	Information and ideas
16	B	Text evidence	Information and ideas
17	B	Multiple texts	Synthesis
18	D	Multiple texts	Synthesis
19	C	Multiple texts	Synthesis

Reading Workout C

1 A The passage is mainly about the boy's experience boarding the ship alone and finding his way to his cabin. The author does not say where the boy is going; in fact, the author implies that the boy himself doesn't know where he's going. He did not even wave at his relatives, so ZAP (B). The adults do talk quietly as they drive the boy to the ship (C), but this is only a detail from the first paragraph, not the focus of the entire passage. Nothing in the passage suggests that there's anything out of the ordinary about the ship's routine (D).

2 A The author spends most of the passage in third-person point of view, telling what the boy is doing and occasionally thinking. In the fourth paragraph, he suddenly shifts to first-person point of view: "I do not know, even now, why he chose this solitude." The boy remains isolated throughout the passage, so ZAP C.

3 D Lines 51–54 are the point at which the author shifts from third-person (*he*) to first-person (*I*). First-person perspective continues through the end of the passage.

4 A The boy seems apathetic throughout the passage, without strong feelings about anything. He neither takes a last look back at the city nor waves at the relatives who are staying behind. We also learn that the boy could have listened to what the adults in the front seat of the car were saying as they took him to the harbor, but he didn't want to. Also, he feels as if there's a wall between himself and the city.

5 C The boy's apathy is demonstrated by the fact that he did not take a last look at the city he was leaving, nor did he choose to wave at the people who brought him to the harbor. A person who cared about either the city or the people would probably have done both of those things.

6 B In lines 26–27, the author says the boy is "green as he could be about the world," meaning he has little life experience or knowledge of the world. He is about to get on "the first and only ship of his life." This indicates that the boy doesn't know what is ahead of him. The harbor is dark, with some lights beginning to come on, but at this point, there's a glow over the city (C). While there's some evidence that the boy feels isolated and alone as he boards the ship, we don't know what waits for him at his destination (D).

7 A Think about what it's like to get into bed. The boy moved easily into the narrow bunk. None of the other choices make sense in the context.

8 C The author says, "The departed [passengers] try to hold on to those disappearing faces until all distinction is lost." Which choice makes the most sense in this context, when people are aboard a ship sailing away, trying to remember the faces of their loved ones? What is lost? It's not *separation* (A); separation is what's happening. It's not marking off (B) or *superiority* (D), which don't make sense in the context. The faces are disappearing from view. When they're gone, the passengers won't be able to see—or recognize—them any longer. All *recognition* is lost.

9 D Before lines 49–51, the author has already told readers that the boy did not go up on deck for a last look or wave at the people he is leaving. He says that in films, people "tear themselves away from one another weeping," and the departing passengers keep looking back until they can't see land anymore. The implication is that such behavior is common (depicted in "films," suggesting more than one). Even the boy can imagine it (lines 51–53). Such departures are in great contrast to the boy's actions; in comparison, his actions are *unusual*.

10 B The author tells us that the boy is 11 years old and that this is "the first and only ship of his life." He doesn't seem to know why things are happening or what will happen next. Like a "little cricket," he's a small creature with no sense of himself in a big, ever-changing world. The word *green* is often used to describe someone young and inexperienced.

11 C The passage starts with Hillary's birth in 1919 and describes major events in his life, concluding with the honors he received in the years leading up to his death in 2008.

12 B The author uses the details about Hillary's life and work to round out the description of Hillary beyond being the first to climb Mount Everest. Hillary received knighthood after returning from Everest. The activities described took place mostly after he was knighted, so they aren't the reason Queen Elizabeth chose to give him that honor (C), although they reinforce his worthiness for such an honor.

13 B In line 47, we read, "Hillary was the first foreign national to receive such an honor...." This is a clue to the meaning of *conferred*. The Nepalese government gave citizenship to Hillary as an honor or gift. The choice closest in meaning to *gave* is *bestowed*.

14 B Although Hillary is most famous for climbing Mount Everest, Nepal honored him also for founding the Himalayan Trust and helping the Sherpa people of Nepal.

15 C The Himalayan Trust built schools and hospitals to help the Sherpa people of Nepal. This is a key reason the Nepalese government conferred honorary citizenship on Hillary.

16 C The paragraph says, "The Picture Library ... covers the world's historic moments" and provides "a glimpse into the world's landscapes, habitats, peoples, and ways of life over time." Because the Society was formed in the same year as the invention of photography, its collection contains pictures of major events that have taken place ever since.

17 A Passage 1 describes the life and accomplishments of Sir Edmund Hillary, an important figure in the history of the Royal Geographical Society. Passage 2 describes the Royal Geographical Society itself. Passage 2 does not continue the discussion of Hillary's life (C). None of the historical information presented in Passage 2 is contradicted by Passage 1 (B). While Passage 2 discusses exploration, it does not directly provide evidence in support of any specific idea introduced in Passage 1 (D).

18 D The mission of the Royal Geographical Society is described in paragraph 2 of Passage 2. It's reasonable to infer that lectures about mountaineering and exploration help advance geographical knowledge in general. It's true that the lecture honors Hillary (B), but that fact doesn't help fulfill the Society's mission.

19 D Lines 53–56 of Passage 1 say that the annual Hillary Memorial Lecture is "usually focused on mountaineering and exploration." The mission of the Royal Geographical Society (discussed in passage 2) is heavily focused on geographical knowledge, which such lectures are likely to promote.

Reading Workout C Item Breakout

ITEM	KEY	SKILL	CONTENT DIMENSION
1	A	Summarizing	Understanding relationships
2	A	Analyzing point of view	Rhetoric
3	D	Textual evidence	Information and ideas
4	A	Close reading	Information and ideas
5	C	Textual evidence	Information and ideas
6	B	Analyzing word choice	Rhetoric
7	A	Words in context	Summarizing
8	C	Words in context	Summarizing
9	D	Understanding relationships	Summarizing
10	B	Analyzing word choice	Rhetoric
11	C	Analyzing text structure	Rhetoric
12	B	Analyzing purpose	Rhetoric
13	B	Words in context	Summarizing
14	B	Close reading	Information and ideas
15	C	Textual evidence	Information and ideas
16	C	Close reading	Information and ideas
17	A	Multiple texts	Synthesis
18	D	Multiple texts	Synthesis
19	D	Textual evidence	Information and ideas

Reading Workout D

1   A   Choices A and B are both true, but only A is addressed in both paragraphs. In the 1700s, arsenic was used for many illnesses, but today it is used mainly to treat a single form of cancer.

2   D   In paragraph 4 of Passage 1, the author says that Britain had no sanitation plans to keep up with garbage and other waste, and then says arsenic was available to kill rats. It's reasonable to infer that the garbage attracted rats, which is why citizens wanted to use arsenic to kill them.

3   B   Lines 26–30 do not explicitly state that rats were once a major nuisance in Britain, but all of the evidence necessary to infer so is found there.

4   B   In line 38 of Passage 1, the author says that arsenic-treated lumber was used "through much of the 20th century." It's possible to infer that the use of such wood was banned at some point after that—relatively recent in comparison to the dates given in choices A, C, and D.

5   C   Because arsenic's uses are more limited today than in the past, most people will only come across mention of arsenic in literary works, such as *Arsenic and Old Lace*, which is still performed by high school and community theater groups.

6   C   The simplest way to answer this question is to plug in each choice in place of *range*. The best fit is *a variety or assortment* (C). There is no mention of any of the others.

7   D   There's no evidence in the passage to support A or C. Because arsenic is naturally occurring, it's not practical for the EPA to eliminate all of it (B). A wide variety of government agencies are mentioned in the passage as monitoring or regulating arsenic (D).

8   C   Up to this point, the passage has offered examples of federal arsenic regulation through OSHA, the EPA, and the FDA. This paragraph mentions that states also regulate arsenic and offers Maryland as an example. There's no evidence for A. While B may be true, it's not the main reason for the author to include it. There's nothing in the passage about D.

9   D   Passage 1 mentions a specific cancer for which arsenic is a treatment and says that further research into medical uses for arsenic is ongoing. Passage 2 says only that the FDA issues guidelines for medicinal use of arsenic. This implies that there are legitimate medical uses for arsenic. Choice A is not mentioned in either passage. C is not stated in Passage 1. B is explicitly stated in both passages.

10   C   The author of Passage 2 mentions that the FDA issues "guidelines for medicinal use" in lines 100–103.

11   B   The first paragraph introduces Professor Barker (D) as well as the construction and novelty of the arc lamp (C). However, the most important purpose of the paragraph is to introduce Edison's passion for improving on the arc lamp ("this electric light idea took possession of me," line 12). Although Edison's telephone project is mentioned in the paragraph (A), that is only to set up the fact that he now has time to investigate electric lighting.

12 D Line 12 expresses Edison's passion for improving on the arc lamp ("this electric light idea took possession of me").

13 A This use of the word *fired* means that Edison liked the idea of the incandescent lamp over the idea of the arc lamp. It's much like saying he was *fired up* by the idea, as one might say today. The passage goes on to describe how Edison and his team worked diligently to find just the right substance for the filament. He was very positive about the incandescent lamp even before finding a solution to the problem. *Excited* is a positive word, and all the other options given are negative, so you can quickly *ZAP* B, C, and D.

14 D By "fishing around and trying all sorts and shapes of things," Edison and his team are being creative. The word *fishing* does not imply that they were *lazy* about their efforts (A). There's nothing indicating that Edison was *ineffective* (B), simply because he tried many different substances. Nor do we have any reason to think that their approach was *tedious* (C). The only thing we know is that they were *creative* because they tried things that had not been tried before.

15 A Edison had a clear vision of the problems with arc lights that would have to be solved. He wasn't trying *to insult* anyone (B) or to *brag* of his invention (C), which didn't exist yet. Arc lights burned too brightly, so choice D also is incorrect.

16 B Edison recounts many of the substances he tried that didn't work. He doesn't do it in a *lighthearted* (A) or *absurd* (C) way, even though he uses the word *funny*. Instead, he seems to indicate that he was surprised that he had previously dismissed carbon only to discover that it worked best of all. There is no evidence to support his being *resentful* (D).

17 A This is an archaic use of the word *answer*, but it's possible to interpret the meaning based on the passage. Edison had tried several other substances that didn't work and recollects what was wrong with each of them. He hadn't thought "that carbon would answer" because of its sensitivity to oxidation. In other words, he hadn't thought it would *work* (A). The other uses of *answer* all refer to a form of speech, something that carbon can't do; *ZAP* them.

18 C The paragraph focuses on the fact that Edison and his team were watching to see how long it would burn (lines 47–48) and were too fascinated to go to bed; however, those lines are not among the choices given. They didn't want to go to bed because at first they were anxious and then they were too elated (lines 54–55). They weren't trying to fall asleep, so were not prevented by *breathlessness* or *brightness* (A and B). Nor were they suffering too much *anxiety*; their anxiety turned to elation (lines 54–55).

19 B Edison states in lines 47–48, "we wanted to see how long it would burn." In order to see how long the lamp would burn, they could not go to sleep. If they did, they might miss recording the exact length of time the lamp burned out. Lines 50–55 also explain that the men were watching the lamp and were too fascinated to go to sleep, but that is not one of the choices given.

Reading Workout D Item Breakout

ITEM	KEY	SKILL	CONTENT DIMENSION
1	A	Understanding relationships	Summarizing
2	D	Close reading	Information and ideas
3	B	Textual evidence	Information and ideas
4	B	Close reading	Information and ideas
5	C	Analyze purpose	Rhetoric
6	C	Words in context	Summarizing
7	D	Understanding relationships	Summarizing
8	C	Analyze text structure	Rhetoric
9	D	Multiple texts	Synthesis
10	C	Multiple texts	Synthesis
11	B	Analyze text structure	Rhetoric
12	D	Textual evidence	Information and ideas
13	A	Words in context	Summarizing
14	D	Close reading	Information and ideas
15	A	Analyze Argument	Rhetoric
16	B	Word choice	Rhetoric
17	A	Words in context	Summarizing
18	C	Central idea	Information and ideas
19	B	Textual evidence	Information and ideas

Reading Workout E

1   A   Near the beginning of the second paragraph, the narrator says, "It was their time together at the beginning of each day and even at an early age I could feel their disappointment if I interrupted them by getting up too early." Of the choices given, A is closest; the narrator knows she shouldn't interrupt, or *distract*, her parents, as they apparently want time to themselves. There is no support for her appearance being considered particularly *pleasant* (B) or *welcome* (C). Yet D (*a rude intrusion*) is too strongly negative; there's no evidence of her parents having harsh feelings about her impending arrival on the scene. She is simply a child waking up too early.

2   D   Lines 46–49 state that early morning was her parents' time together, and the narrator "could feel their disappointment if I interrupted them by getting up too early."

3   B   Earlier in the passage, the narrator talks about a flight (set) of stairs (A), but that's not the meaning at this point in the passage. She dreams she is "on the roof … on tiptoe, arms outstretched in the position for flight"—much like a bird might be when taking off. When she jumps "out my fifty-story-high window into the black lake of sky," she is able to "look inside the homes of people who interested me." She can choose where she goes, so choice D (*freefalling*) is incorrect. She is an individual child, not a group of *birds* (C). *Soaring* is another word for *flying* and is closest in meaning to the word *flight*.

4   A   Lines 7–8 say the narrator had recurring dreams that she could fly.

5   B   After writing, "In the kitchen they would be discussing events in the barrio," she says that her father "would be carrying that part of the conversation." The narrator explains that her mother would talk about "her desire to see her *familia* on the Island." In other words, her father would talk about the barrio, while her mother would talk about visiting her family.

6   D   The narrator is a 12-year-old girl who likes to *imagine* herself flying across the sky, peering in on people she knows. Each morning, she "would stay in my bed recalling my dreams of flight, perhaps planning my next flight." There's no evidence that she is *unhappy* (A), *lonely* (B), or *impatient* (C).

7   B   We know that the narrator's mother wants to take a vacation in Puerto Rico. She talks about going to the beach. Then she looks out the kitchen window to see a narrow alley filled with refuse. "She'd sigh deeply and say the same thing the view from her kitchen window always inspired her to say," which the footnote translates to: "Oh, if I could fly." It makes sense that seeing the refuse-filled alley would make her sad and *long for* Puerto Rico. There's no evidence in the text to support A, C, or D.

8   D   When the narrator's mother would talk about going to Puerto Rico, her husband "would answer patiently, gently." In other words, he was *caring*. There's no evidence in the text to support A, B, or C.

9   A   The narrator dreams of flying freely through the sky looking at people she is "obsessed" with, while her mother wishes she could fly to visit the family and home she misses. Both the narrator and her mother dream of the freedom to go where they wish to be. Even though the narrator's father reminds his wife that they can't afford to go to the Island, there's no talk of the *dangers of dreaming* (B). The mother appears to be sad at *living far from her family* (C), but that has no bearing on why the narrator dreams of flying. Although the father discusses events in the barrio, there is no talk of the uncertainties of life in the barrio (D).

10   C   Three significant periods of drought have occurred since 2000, covering a majority of the years since the turn of the century. Although wetter periods occurred between them, times of abundant rainfall are growing shorter. So are periods of relatively normal rainfall between the wettest and driest years.

11   A   Lines 24–28 mention three lengthy periods of drought followed by wetter periods that became shorter with less time between them than in previous years.

12   C   In paragraph 5, the author cautions readers that direct comparisons of the current drought to previous droughts are challenging, and then he/she lists reasons why. Because of the unique conditions under which the drought is occurring, it cannot necessarily be compared to earlier droughts without taking the current conditions into consideration.

13   A   Paragraph 4 describes conditions during the 1975–1977 drought and says, "water shortages were exceptional." The mention of the water pipeline constructed across a bridge in the Bay Area is intended to illustrate just how exceptional the shortages were.

14   C   Although the closing paragraph follows a long historical discussion, it does not summarize any *longitudinal data* (A). Although the author warns that PDSI should not be the only factor in evaluating a drought, there's no argument against *drawing premature conclusions* (B.) The closing paragraph describes the environmental and economic impact of the current drought and explains why the governor issued a state of emergency. It does not *criticize* that policy (D). Instead, it is a description of *current challenges* at the time the article was written.

15   C   The last paragraph of the passage discusses the impact of the drought on the environment and the economy of California, and says that the governor issued a state of emergency in response. This indicates that the impacts of the drought are *greatly significant*.

16   D   Graph 2 contains year-by-year information regarding the Palmer Drought Severity Index (PDSI), which is compiled by the National Climatic Data Center (NCDC). For this reason, the graph is not a *rebuttal to* NCDC's historical information (A)—it *is* NCDC's historical information. Although the recent PDSI index shows severe drought, it does not *prove* that the current drought *crisis cannot be solved* (C). Neither is the information *peripheral to the drought information* presented in the passage (B). The PDSI figures allow the reader to visualize the drought's *severity*, although the author cautions that it's only one value used to compare one drought to another.

17 D The PDSI is useful for comparing the severity of one drought to another as explained in lines 59–64.

18 B The jagged line represents yearly precipitation. The highest peak is found between 1980 and 1989.

19 B The precise way to interpret PDSI is never stated in the passage, but the passage lists several years of severe drought, which correspond to negative PDSI numbers. This makes it possible to infer that the more strongly negative a PDSI is, the worse a drought is. To confirm this inference, compare rainfall statistics from graph 1 to PDSI in graph 2. In strongly negative PDSI years, rainfall amounts are lower than less negative or positive PDSI years.

Reading Workout E Item Breakout

ITEM	KEY	SKILL	CONTENT DIMENSION
1	A	Close reading	Information and ideas
2	D	Textual evidence	Information and ideas
3	B	Words in context	Summarizing
4	A	Textual evidence	Information and ideas
5	B	Central idea	Information and ideas
6	D	Central idea	Information and ideas
7	B	Close reading	Information and ideas
8	D	Close reading	Information and ideas
9	A	Analyzing purpose	Rhetoric
10	C	Close reading	Information and ideas
11	A	Textual evidence	Information and ideas
12	C	Analyzing arguments	Rhetoric
13	A	Analyzing purpose	Rhetoric
14	C	Analyzing arguments	Rhetoric
15	C	Words in context	Summarizing
16	D	Quantitative information	Synthesis
17	D	Textual evidence	Information and ideas
18	B	Quantitative information	Synthesis
19	B	Quantitative information	Synthesis

Reading Workout F

1 C The first paragraph describes a glowing, luminous, 4,000-year-old treasure of gold and silver from one of the most famous of all ancient cities. A reader might easily find it *awe-inspiring* that any item can last so long. Permanence in itself can't be *vile* (A) or *horrifying* (D). While you might consider 4,000 years to be an *extreme* period of time (B), consider how the author describes the Aline Kilmer quote as a reflection on "how everyday items as well as precious artworks can survive centuries after their owners are dead and forgotten."

2 B "The terrible permanence of things" refers to the awe-inspiring ways in which ancient artifacts are able to survive through the centuries. The writer says, "We owe [their survival] to human persistence, daring, deceit, greed, and love of beauty."

3 C All of the choices are true statements, but just because something is true that doesn't make it a correct answer. When Schliemann found the treasure, he assumed it belonged to Priam. Only later was the treasure discovered to be from an earlier time in history, a thousand years before events of the Trojan War were supposed to have taken place.

4 B Lines 44–46 correct Schliemann's mistaken assumption.

5 A Under international law, artifacts found after 1970 can't be removed from their country of origin; but that doesn't apply to the Treasure of Priam, which was unearthed in the late 19th century. Still, Germany's right to the treasure (B) is questionable, as Turkey also claims it. The treasure was found in Turkey, causing that country to claim ownership (A). The treasure actually *predates* the Trojan War by about 1000 years (C). Schliemann's agreement obligated him to give only half of the treasure to Turkey (D). Whether he should have given such priceless treasures to Turkey anyway is a matter of opinion, not a fact. Counterarguments to this opinion are given in the next-to-last paragraph of the passage.

6 D The passage describes the complicated journey of the ancient Treasure of Priam from its discovery during the 19th century to the present. The passage touches on topics mentioned in choices A, B, and C, but none of them is a main focus of the passage.

Be prepared for college-level words like *convoluted* in questions and answer choices. Though the SAT claims to test only commonly used vocabulary as vocabulary words, there are many other places in the test where you may see higher-level words. The best way to improve your vocabulary is to read a lot. Another good way is to get an app to help you learn vocabulary. A strong vocabulary will help you in life well beyond your high school years.

7 A The author's appreciation for the Treasure of Priam is evident throughout the article. She takes no position of approval or disapproval of the actions of Schliemann versus the government of Turkey (B), or the actions of the governments of Germany and Russia. She also takes no position on the honesty or dishonesty of archaeologists and museums today (C) or whether the treasure should be returned to Turkey and/or Egypt (D).

8 B Egypt and Turkey see these items in foreign museums, but they want their treasures returned because they *believe* the treasures are an important part of their cultures.

9 D Although the Treasure of Priam was kept safe in an underground bunker in Germany during World War II, the war put the treasure at risk. After the war, Russian soldiers took the Treasure of Priam from Germany and shipped them to Russia, where they were held covertly until 1993. The other arguments are all claimed in the passage, and they may or may not be valid. There is, however, no evidence in the passage that directly contradicts them.

10 D In paragraph 3, the author says that the advent of electric pumping in the 1940s increased grain and cattle farming, and the irrigation required for these types of farming depletes the water supply more quickly. Choices A, B, and C may or may not be true, but they aren't mentioned in the passage as a cause of the diminished water supply.

11 B Lines 37–42 explain that after 1940, electric pumping made possible more water-intensive farming practices (irrigation), which led to quicker depletion of the aquifer.

12 A By showing how extensively all people depend on groundwater, the author hopes to show that the threat to the Ogallala Aquifer from depletion is cause for concern.

13 A The author suggests that "ominously," even Nebraska, which is in comparatively better shape with its water table, may find itself in jeopardy. The "serious problem" of consistently falling water tables described in paragraph 4 is called a "looming crisis" in paragraph 5. These words are intended to suggest that the current water problems in the region might be getting worse.

14 C The paragraph containing line 77 discusses steps farmers are taking to reduce the amount of water they use. They are trying to slow, or *restrain*, the depletion of the aquifer.

15 A See the next-to-last paragraph in the passage. The author describes several methods with which farmers are trying to conserve water: planting crops that need less water and using irrigation systems or farming methods that conserve water. But while this might save some water, some question whether it will keep the water level in the aquifer from decreasing further.

16 C After describing the water-conserving farming methods, the author remarks in lines 76–78 that "some question whether, or how well, these measures can stem the depletion of the aquifer." Not everyone believes such methods will work as hoped.

17 D The passage deals generally with the problem of aquifer depletion and specifically with the challenges facing farmers on the Great Plains. But because a large percentage of Americans everywhere depend on groundwater for daily life, the author illustrates the seriousness of the problem with scenarios anyone anywhere can relate to.

18 D Consider whether each choice is supported by the graph before choosing your answer. Choice A is not supported because there's no evaluation in the table about how critical any state's situation is. We only know the water level compared to the baseline, not whether the status poses a problem for any given state. South Dakota had a higher-than-baseline water level for several years; however, Nebraska also had higher-than-baseline levels in 2000, 2002, and 2011, so B is not supported. C is incorrect because Colorado dropped 10.1', and Kansas dropped 14.6'. Both are greater than the 7.5' drop experienced by Texas. Choice D is the last one left after the others have been eliminated, but it's easy to verify: The figures for Kansas get slightly lower every year since 2000, indicating a continuous drop.

19 B To find this answer, look for figures that are positive and the same or greater than the previous year. From 2012 to 2013, 2008 to 2009, and 2006 to 2007, there was just one state that had its water levels stay steady or increase (South Dakota in each year); from 2010 to 2011, there were two (Nebraska and South Dakota).

Reading Workout F Item Breakout

ITEM	KEY	SKILL	CONTENT DIMENSION
1	C	Words in context	Summarizing
2	B	Text structure	Rhetoric
3	C	Close reading	Information and ideas
4	B	Textual evidence	Information and Ideas
5	A	Close reading	Information and ideas
6	D	Central idea	Information and ideas
7	A	Analyze purpose	Rhetoric
8	B	Words in context	Summarizing
9	D	Analyze argument	Rhetoric
10	D	Understanding relationships	Summarizing
11	B	Textual evidence	Information and ideas
12	A	Analyze argument	Rhetoric
13	A	Word choice	Rhetoric
14	C	Words in context	Summarizing
15	A	Close reading	Information and ideas
16	C	Textual evidence	Information and ideas
17	D	Analyze point of view	Rhetoric
18	D	Quantitative information	Synthesis
19	B	Quantitative information	Synthesis

Doorway to College
FOUNDATION
Supporting the transition to higher education™

PRODUCT GUIDE

STUDY SKILLS

Study Smart! Classes

Study Smart! Study Skills Recording

Study Skills for Classroom Tests E-book

TEST PREP

ZAPS ACT Seminars, Webinars, and Recordings

ZAPS PSAT/SAT Seminars, Webinars, and Recordings

ACT Subtest Intensive Instructional Videos

ZAPS Online ACT or SAT Practice Test

ZAPS College Vocabulary Challenge App

Tame Test Anxiety: Confidnece Training for Teens

Personal Best Test Training (PBTT) Seminars and Webinars

COLLEGE PREP

Writing an Exceptional College Entrance Essay E-book

Interviewing: In the Hot Seat E-book

College Applications E-book

Making the Most of Your College Visit E-book

College Admissions Essay E-book

Kickstart to College Workshops 1 + 2

STUDENT ATHLETE

#1: Goal Setting for Student Athletes E-book

#2: The Division Decision E-book

#3: The Road to Playing College Sports E-book

#4: How to Succeed as a College Athlete E-book

> *Use promo code* **doorway2college** *to receive a 10% discount on digital products!*

 877-927-8378   prep@doorwaytocollege.com   Doorway to College   @Doorway2College   www.doorwaytocollege.com

→ page 82-83

{ look at Kitchen conversions }

→ fill in all the spaces you can for grid-in's

E1: can't believe I did that! → Slow Down!

E2: I can't remeber → re-learn/review!!!

E3: I don't know that → don't worry, ï → ü

SAT {
Writing
Reading
Math
Secret 4th
}

find the most
interesting first & Annotate

ACT {
English
Math
Reading
Science
}

→ page {92} → stay active while you read

ACT ⇒ 1. Charts & Graphs   ACTstudent.org/scie
Science in   2. Reading Passage
order   3. Experiments